T0079711

OLIVE

Edible

Series Editor: Andrew F. Smith

EDIBLE is a revolutionary series of books dedicated to food and drink that explores the rich history of cuisine. Each book reveals the global history and culture of one type of food or beverage.

Already published

Olive

A Global History

Fabrizia Lanza

REAKTION BOOKS

Published by Reaktion Books Ltd
Unit 32, Waterside
44–48 Wharf Road
London N1 7UX, UK
www.reaktionbooks.co.uk

First published 2011, reprinted 2017

Printed and bound in China by 1010 Printing International Ltd

British Library Cataloguing in Publication Data

Lanza, Fabrizia
Olive: a global history. – (Edible)
1. Olive. 2. Olive – History.
3. Cooking (Olives)
4. Olive – Folklore.
I. Title II. Series
641.3 463-DC22

ISBN 978 1 86189 868 5

Contents

Introduction

The olive's history is almost as ancient as that of humanity itself. An olive tree does not reach its full productivity for 35 years and it is a plant that can endure for centuries. Who was the first person patient enough to wait those three decades? Whoever he – or she – was, we know that the olive has been growing alongside human beings from time immemorial. It lives in our literature, it is part of our symbolism, it lights our prayers and it enriches both our culture and our diet.

The wild species of the plant seems to have been discovered at least 10,000 years BCE, and the domesticated version appeared some 4,000 years ago. It is a story that goes back at least to the beginnings of agriculture, when human beings first settled down and began to cultivate the earth and harvest its fruits. To trace in just one brief volume the long, long story of the olive, its symbolic significance and the technical skills that had to be mastered in order to press the oil and cure the olives, is thus to undertake a voyage 6,000 years long. It is an entertaining voyage, during which an almost infinite number of tales and legends emerge, a multitude of customs and traditions that belong to many different places and civilizations. These cultures may be far away from our own in time and place but they all attributed to the olive a high, even regal status, a value well beyond the plant's dietary or cosmetic uses.

Homer, Virgil, Cato, Pliny, Aristophanes, Dante, Shakespeare, Frédéric Mistral, Van Gogh, Calvino: many poets, scientists, artists and historians have admired the olive tree, granting it the status of a genuine icon of the Western world. To be born under an olive tree was a mark of divine ancestry: the twins Artemis and Apollo as well as Romulus and Remus, descended from the gods, were born under an olive tree. Olive wood, signalling endurance and quality, often appears during Odysseus' endless travels: his bed is carved from an ancient olive tree, the stick thrust into the Cyclops' eye is made of olive wood, and so is the handle of the axe with which he builds his boat.

From time immemorial, anointing oneself with oil has been the preferred way to approach the hereafter. Unguents, mixtures of oils and spices, were sacred to the Babylonians and to the prophets of the Bible; they were essential during the burial of ancient Greek athletes and warriors; and they played an integral role in the Christian sacraments. In the Middle Ages, holy oil, precious and deeply sacred, was said to flow directly from the bones of Christian martyrs. Almost as powerful in modern times is the way imported olive oil subtly conveyed a sense of identity to European immigrants in the United States, satisfying, along with their appetites for flavours from home, their nostalgia and other intangible desires.

An overview of these six millennia of history must obviously begin with a brief excursus on the olive tree itself, from pre-history to modern times – a multiform and complicated story of the ships that sailed the waves of the Mediterranean back and forth, first from East to West, and slowly conquered all of Europe. The second chapter traces the symbolic role the olive and its oil have always played, from rituals in Egyptian and Etruscan tombs, to the Christian sacraments, to the rituals celebrated in the past century in Provence and central Italy during the olive harvest. A third chapter is dedicated to the history of oil extraction – from the earliest mortars in which the olives were crushed, to primitive presses, often of industrial dimensions even in ancient times, to the more sophisticated machines of the nineteenth century. Curiously enough, the knowledge and skills related to olive cultivation, harvest and pressing that were accumulated by the ancient Romans and lost for centuries during the Middle Ages reemerged, like an underground spring, in modern times. In the fourth chapter I write about the olive's migration to the New World with the arrival of the Spanish empire in South America. Once the olive had established itself in the fertile soils of California, it was largely the immigrants from Mediterranean countries who took charge of it, delighted to have this memory of home in a far-away land. The book concludes with some questions about the Mediterranean Diet, those dietary recommendations that, beginning in the 1950s, brought with them a new idea about the beneficial effects of olive oil. Could it be that behind this newfound passion for olive oil there are motivations that go far beyond the dietetic and medical arguments made by scientists, doctors and dietary experts? Are there more profound reasons why we favour olive oil? These are tantalizing questions.

There are many, many recipes made with olive oil, somewhat fewer that employ the olive fruit. In giving recipes I've taken a thematic approach, offering cross-country comparisons of how olive oil becomes the base for a sauce, for example: to make aioli in Provence, or pesto in Liguria. Bread dipped in oil is a basic element of the Mediterranean Diet, whether it is called *bruschetta* in Rome, *brissa* in Nice or *fettunta* in Tuscany. Finally, olive oil is still the preferred fat in some traditional Southern European sweets and desserts, a custom that gives

Cassatelle, Sicilian ricotta-stuffed pastries made with olive oil. For recipe, see pp. 104–5.

Broccoli with black olives. For recipe, see p. 100.

these dishes a decidedly Mediterranean texture and a flavour that is far from French-style *patisserie* made with butter.

And so our travels, begun thousands of years ago between the Tigris and the Euphrates, bring us to the *cassatelle* of Sicily, the *melomakarona* of Greece. To Australia, to Asia: where will the olive take us next?

I

The Ancient Roots of the Olive

The entire Mediterranean seems to rise out of the sour, pungent
taste of black olives between the teeth. A taste older than meat
and wine, a taste as old as cold water. Only the sea itself seems as
ancient a part of the region as the olives and its oil, that like no
other products of nature, have shaped civilisations from remotest
antiquity to the present.

Laurence Durrell, *Prospero's Cell*

It isn't easy to identify the precise moment when the wild
olive or *oleaster*, a spiny, ungainly bush, first appeared. Wild
olives were certainly growing all along the Mediterranean
coast many thousands of years ago. Olive stones from the
Paleolithic era have been found in southern France, the Pyr-
enees and Germany. An olive stone unearthed in Spain has
been carbon-dated to 6000 BCE.

The *oleaster*, with its tiny black inedible berries, bears no
resemblance to *Olea europea*, the domesticated olive tree with
its pulpy, translucent fruits and majestic allure. *O. europea* can
tolerate long periods of drought but not too much cold and
not for long periods. It will grow happily where temperatures
do not fall below 12°F (-8°C) and at an altitude which varies
according to latitude: in Sicily olives grow on Mount Etna up

The best olive oil is made from olives that have been harvested when still unripe.

Olea europaea var. sylvestris

to 900 m above sea level, while in central Italy they are not found above 300 to 400 m. According to the rules laid down by the ancient Greek scientist Theophrastus, olives should never be cultivated more than 53 kilometres from the sea; thus they can be found nearly everywhere around the Mediterranean.

As for where and when *O. europea* was domesticated for the first time, we do not know for sure, but it is reasonable to think that took place somewhere near the Fertile Crescent where human beings first domesticated plants and animals. This stretch of land around the Tigris and Euphrates rivers runs west through Syria to Lebanese shores, and south toward the African desert, where the land is periodically irrigated by the flood waters of the Nile.[1]

The most ancient evidence of olive domestication, cultivation and trade has been found in the regions of Syria, Palestine and Crete. From what we know, olive cultivation developed independently in these three places. The linguistic spread of the two main words which have designated the olive since ancient times – the Greek *elea* and the Semitic *zeit* – supports this theory.[2] The various names of olives and olive oil around the Mediterranean derive from those two words: we find *elea* and its occidental translation, *olea*, all over Europe and the Western world. Meanwhile the Semitic word *zeit*, traceable to Syria, was adopted by the Egyptians and then by the Arabs, who spread it widely with their conquest.

Whatever the precise place of origin, it was along the dry and sunny shores of the Mediterranean Sea that the olive tree grew leafy and prosperous. When the Flood recounted in the Bible ended, a dove carrying an olive branch appeared to Noah as a sign that the deluge was finished (Genesis 8:11).

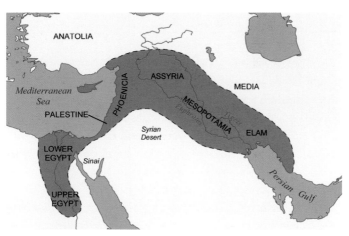

The Fertile Crescent.

Olive tree, Sicily.

This and numerous other biblical references to olive trees and olive oil suggest that long before the Bible was composed olive trees were probably already growing on Mount Ararat and were cultivated by Semitic peoples. In the second millennium BCE, not far from Mount Ararat, Prince Hammurabi of the Babylonian Empire laid down very strict rules regarding commerce in olive oil, indicating that the olive already had great economic significance.

Moving west to archaic Greece, around 3500 BCE, what was probably a wilder version of the tree we know today was also intensively cultivated on the island of Crete. After 2000 BCE, olive oil began to play a major role in the island's economy as the tree's cultivation expanded and became more systematic. In the Knossos palace, identified as the home of the fabled Minotaur, large deposits of enormous *pithoi* (amphorae), two metres high and used for oil storage, have been found. In the ancient Cretan city of Phaistos, excavators have found remains of an olive press and clay tablets that were marked with the provenance and destination of the oil, which was sold all over the Mediterranean and especially to Egypt. Areas such as this, devoted to the storage of olive oil and its commerce, demonstrate that oil was one of the pillars of the Minoan economic system on Crete.

Still farther west, in Egypt, under the reign of Ramses II, (1279–1212/13 BCE) we find a record of the donations made in oil produced from an olive grove measuring 2,700 hectares. This plantation was near the town of Heliopolis, and the oil produced was donated to the sun-god Ra to light his sanctuaries. In Ramses' tomb as well as in that of Tutankhamen (c. 1325 BCE) surviving frescoes depict vases of olive oil, luxurious provisions for the soul's voyage to the other world.

Olive trees in the traditional Garden of Gethsemane, on the Mount of Olives.

The same was true in Greece and Palestine, where olive oil was held in high esteem: Homer, in the *Odyssey*, gives perfumed olive oil a ritual value when he tells of the meeting between Odysseus and Princess Nausicaa, daughter of Alcinous. Odysseus, having reached the shore after a thunderstorm and completely covered with salt, is washed and prepared for his meeting with Nausicaa and anointed with olive oil. It is interesting to note that both Homer and Hesiod knew about olive trees and olive oil and were able to distinguish the wild tree from the cultivated (*Odyssey* 5:477). Nevertheless, they mostly refer to the olive as a single tree, and for them oil was a perfumed balm for the body, never a substance used in cooking or for food.

It was in Palestine that the domestication of olive trees and the production of olive oil reached levels never obtained before in the pre-industrial age. There, an oil press (recently excavated near Tel Aviv) was capable of producing up to 2,000 tons of oil a year. This oil was for lighting and for cosmetic purposes, and was exported to the Nile region for embalming and Egyptian funeral rites. In Tel Mique-Ekron, a few kilometres from Jerusalem, a huge mill for processing olives that contained a hundred presses has been dated to 1000 BCE and is thought to be one of the largest industrial complexes of antiquity.

The oil produced by the Palestinians was then transported by the Phoenicians with their fast ships throughout the Mediterranean, beyond Egypt to Cyrenaica, and past Carthage, competing with the colonists of Magna Graecia for the markets of Sicily, Sardinia and the Spanish coast. We know that Phoenician colonists took olive trees with them to the Iberian Peninsula around 800 BCE, and they may have introduced the olive tree to Sicily and from there, skipping along the shores of the Mediterranean, to other places in Europe and North

A clay skyphos (two-handled wine cup) depicting the owl, symbol of Athena, surrounded by olive branches, 4th century BCE, Puglia.

Africa. By the eighth century olives and olive oil were well established along the length and breadth of the Mediterranean.

By this time, the importance of the olive tree in the Greek economy was such that the olive had acquired a mythical status. In a very famous Greek tale, Athena and Poseidon were competing for supremacy in Attica. Before the council of gods, the two had to think of a gift to give the region. Poseidon gave a white horse and with a violent gesture created a salted lake. Athena gave birth to an olive tree on the highest hill in the region. The people chose Athena's gift and named their city after her. According to legend, during the Persian invasion of 480 BCE the olive tree on the Acropolis burned down. But the next day the tree put out a new shoot and was still alive in the second century.

From then onward, Athena's gift became a sort of national symbol in ancient Greece, with olive leaves impressed on coins, and wreaths of olive branches awarded to the athlete who won the Hecatombaion, a major competition held every

A sard seal-stone engraved with an athlete, nude except for drapery over his right arm, holding an olive branch; a draped Victory crowns him with an olive wreath, 323 BCE–31 BCE.

four years after 556 BCE in Athena's honour. The prizes for the pan-Athenian games included money, gold and silver medals and large decorated amphorae containing olive oil.[3] The sacred olive trees harvested to produce the olive oil for the competition were protected under special laws. An Archon and an Areopagus, high-up officials, looked after the trees and collected the olives, and it was severely forbidden to cut or damage the sacred trees.

By this time the Greek colonies in Sicily and along the Ionian coast, like Tarantum and Sybaris, and as far west as Marseilles, had begun producing olive oil and were soon competing with the homeland in quality and quantity. Boats loaded with amphorae full of olive oil continually plied the Mediterranean.

The planting of olive trees and the use of olive oil spread to central Italy from the Greek colonies in Italy – probably from Sicily – between the eighteenth and fifth centuries BCE. In inland Italy, along the Apennines from the Po plain in the north to Benevento in the south, the Etruscans began growing the olive tree. Although these regions may have cultivated olives previously, olives and olive oil now became one of their main products, and in just a few decades the Etruscan elite, learning from Greece and especially from Attica, started using new products and ingredients and developed new eating habits. Wine was adopted during the symposium (from the Greek word *sunpinein*, which means 'drink together'), where philosophical discussions were enhanced by calibrated doses of alcohol. The wealthiest Etruscans, considering olive oil a great luxury, used it mainly as a cosmetic, for burial uses and for lighting. Around the end of the seventh century the Etruscans started cultivating their own olive trees and making their own oil. At that point, olive oil was no longer a costly product and was within the reach of all. It is probably for this reason that Etruscan tombs from this period contain an ever increasing number of tiny oil ampoules and oil lamps. And it was from the Etruscans that the Romans, under Tarquinius Priscus' reign, learned how to harvest grapes and make wine, how to cultivate the olive tree, how to judge when the olives were ready for the harvest and what methods to use to press the olives and produce the best oil.

As the empire grew the Romans planted olives across Europe, and wherever the climate allowed the plant to grow, it has remained. Pliny the Elder, who in the first century BCE wrote extensively about olives and oil in his *Natural History*, records that beginning in the first century BCE the Roman Empire was the largest olive oil producer in Europe and that different varieties of olives were being cultivated as far north as Gaul and as far west as Spain.[4] His description of different grades of olive oil is still valid and demonstrates the great interest the Romans had in olive oil not only as a balm, but also, in time, as an important enrichment when cooking and serving food.

As the Empire expanded, Italian oil production proved insufficient, and Rome needed more olive oil to satisfy her demand. Olive oil began to be imported from the provinces of the Empire as a tax payment. Plutarch would praise Caesar for the African conquest because it assured Rome three million litres of oil per year.

Mount Testaccio is a living monument to this olive oil trade and distribution. It is an artificial hill near the centre of Rome, some 40 metres high and about 2 hectares wide, that rose out of all the remains of olive oil amphorae that had arrived in Rome between the first and second century BCE. By counting the number of amphorae in Testaccio, we can conclude that more than 320,000 amphorae were arriving in Rome each year during the imperial age, the equivalent of 22,480 tons. Considering that Rome had by that time one million inhabitants, each would have consumed about two litres of olive oil per month, a great deal by the standards of today. But of course we have to remember that oil was used not only for food but also for lighting, body care, medicine and engineering.[5]

After the collapse of the Roman Empire the cultivation of olive trees began to decline. The warm climate that had accompanied the growth of the Roman Empire was now changing, and with colder weather northern populations began to move south. It was now too cold to grow olive trees in northern countries. Rome was gradually losing control of the provinces, and of its olive plantations. Italy was under constant invasion by new populations coming from the north in search of land and a better climate. An age of war, devastation and famine began; trade became impossible. The countryside was no longer a safe place to live, as barbarian invaders devastated all that stood in their path. Olive plantations were abandoned; the population, afraid to move, simply tried to hide away.

The invading populations had different habits and their own agricultural traditions, and they imposed a new diet on their Roman descendants. Many brought with them a taste for beer, lard, meat and milk, from a world of hunting and forests where olive oil was not produced. For them, olive oil probably tasted strong and acidic compared with the sweetness of butter. Soon the Romans' neat farms and vegetable gardens, their intensive cultivation of vines and olive trees, were abandoned and grew up into woodland. Olive oil was still to be found, but it had once again become an expensive ingredient available mainly to the aristocracy and to the upper ecclesiastical ranks.

Meanwhile new invaders from the south, the Arabs, were extending their dominion across Africa and into Europe. They seem to have had little interest in planting and spreading the olive, and they probably got most of their oil from the extensive North African groves first established by the Romans. Al-Idrisi (1099–1165/6), one of the most celebrated geographers at the Norman court of Roger II in Palermo, wrote a report on the varieties of plants growing in the king's territory,

Olive tree on the island of Pantelleria, Italy; the branches, held down by weights, grow along the ground where they are protected from the wind.

but he did not mention olives, except to say he had only seen them on the island of Pantelleria, south of Sicily.

We shall have to wait until after the year 1000 for olive oil to be rediscovered, and for new olive plantations to arise. Against the 'barbarian' culture of lard and meat, monasteries and the Church promoted and protected a counter-culture based on olive oil. Christians respected fasting laws and did not eat animal fat – butter, suet or lard – for much of the year. Fasting became more than a rule the faithful must abide by: it became a symbol of identity, a mark of belonging, a way for the Christian community to show the antiquity of its roots and to claim its descent from the Roman culture of the first Christian martyrs.

The olive tree, which until then had been secreted behind the walls of monasteries, protected by the Church and used for lighting and to impart the sacraments, seems now to have become fashionable. According to scholars like Massimo Montanari,[6] the new oil culture appealed to Europeans, as did that new religion, Christianity, which was now beginning to be propagated in a Europe that still had a largely pagan soul.

Later, olive oil would cease to be a status symbol or a mark of religious and cultural identity. It simply became part of the diet and culinary habits of Italy, southern France and Spain: the highest-ranking condiment in a culture of vegetables and salads. Giacomo Castelvetro, born in the Italian region of Emilia and exiled to London at the beginning of the seventeenth century because he was a Protestant, considered vegetables seasoned with olive oil a distinctive feature of his homeland, for which he felt deep nostalgia. In 1614 he even wrote a little treatise on the matter, addressed to his London hosts: *Brieve racconto di tutte le radici, di tutte l'erbe e di tutti i frutti che crudi o cotti in Italia si mangiano* ('A brief account of all the roots, all the herbs and all the fruits, both raw and cooked, eaten in Italy').

Before the olive became part of the diet, however, it was already a mainstay of trade. Travellers at the end of the thirteenth century who ventured south to the land of Bari and Otranto, in today's Italian region of Puglia, observed that the landscape was thick with olive trees. Venice would soon develop an important industry importing oil from Puglia to make soap and provide lamp oil along the Adriatic coast, as well as to sell to northern Europe.[7] Olive oil became indispensable in the production of soaps and, via strict laws protecting its control of the trade, the Venetian Republic was able to impose itself politically and economically across northern Italy. New boats, called *marciliane*, were built for oil transportation: very light, with a flat base, these boats were able to transport hundreds of barrels of olive oil at a time.

While Venice was consolidating its power in northern Italy trading soap and olive oil, Florence was developing new textile products which would become sought after across

'Olive', from *The Tudor Pattern Book*, English manuscript, *c.* 1520–30.

Europe. Paris, Bruges, Antwerp, Flanders, London: to all these places Florence would export its high-quality linens, silks, cottons and wools, together with wines and olive oil. In Florence olive oil was used to oil the fibres and to comb the fabrics, because it is the only fat which remains liquid at room temperature. Because the hills of Tuscany did not provide enough oil for the textile workshops, they needed to purchase oil in the south of Italy: from Calabria, Campania and, when Venice consented, a small portion of the oil from Puglia.

During the Renaissance, oil from southern Italy came to be fundamental in industry and for lighting. With strong demand coming from all European markets, Venice was in charge of olive oil supplies from Puglia, while Genoa managed those from Calabria, along with the Tuscans, Russians, Germans,

Dutch and English. Monks from the Cistercian and Olivetani orders transformed the rocky land at the tip of Puglia above Capo di Leuca into vast olive plantations. A constant traffic of foreign ships filled every harbour in the region. In the coastal Puglia town of Gallipoli, diplomatic legations from all over Europe set up offices, and many consulates remained there right up to 1923. The peak of olive oil production in Puglia and Calabria corresponded to the high point of the wool industry in Florence in the fourteenth century; it then peaked again in the seventeenth century with sales to England and Flanders.

The big chill of 1709 was one of the worst in historical record. The entire south of Europe – Greece, the Balkans, Italy, most of France and even Spain – was hit by the freeze and most of the olive trees died or were abandoned. Tuscany alone increased its olive groves, but the region only managed to match the quantity produced before the chill after the mid-eighteenth century. It was in this period that Tuscany started specializing in producing high-quality oil for cooking, while southern Italy took the opposite path, choosing to emphasize quantity and mostly producing lamp oil. Italian oil, both comestible and for lighting, now found markets all across Europe as far as Russia.

As the eighteenth century came to a close, much of Italy was covered with olive groves. Other olive oils, whether they came from Provence, Greece, Spain or North Africa, offered only weak competition to the Italian products. The crunch would only come with the appearance of new oils and greases for use in manufacturing during the century of the Industrial Revolution.

In the second half of the nineteenth century olive oil production stopped expanding. The climate proved unstable and there were repeated freezes, culminating in a catastrophic one in 1929. By the beginning of the twentieth century production had begun to contract. The period was one of heavy emigration, with a corresponding sharp decline in the labour force, particularly in the south. Fields and orchards were abandoned as farmers went abroad to seek their fortunes and the olive trees were left to look after themselves. Meanwhile those Italians who went abroad to the United States, Australia and New Zealand introduced the cultivation of the olive tree and began to spread the habit of cooking and dressing foods with olive oil. It was the beginning of a new story – a love story between the olive and the New World.

2

Ointments, Anointments and Holy Oil: The Olive in Ritual

I bring no overture of war, no taxation of homage; I hold the
olive in my hand: my words are as full of peace as matter.

William Shakespeare, *Twelfth Night*, Act 1 Scene 5

And here there grows, unpruned, untamed,
Terror to foemen's spear,
A tree in Asian soil unnamed,
By Pelops' Dorian isle unclaimed,
Self-nurtured year by year;
'Tis the grey-leaved olive that feeds our boys;
Nor youth nor withering age destroys
The plant that the Olive Planter tends
And the Grey-eyed Goddess herself defends.

Sophocles, *Oedipus at Colonus*

Why do the olive tree and its products have such immense
symbolic value in all the civilizations that have flourished
around the Mediterranean? The significance of the olive goes
far beyond its basic uses in lighting, cosmetics and food
preparation. Together with wheat and wine, the olive tree
makes up a trinity that marks a cultural identity, a cultural
universe, that is not always consistent with geographical

An olive tree can live for up to 3,000 years. In Sardinia and Puglia there are still large plantations of ancient olive trees.

boundaries. It marks a long and nearly uninterrupted line linking various different civilizations across several millennia of history. Not surprisingly the great French historian Fernand Braudel considered the olive tree as *the* distinguishing feature of the Mediterranean itself.[1]

It can't be incidental to the olive's symbolic power that it takes a long time to grow an olive tree, and that an olive is almost eternal. As the Italian proverb puts it: *Vigna piantata da me; moro da mio padre. Olivo da mio nonno.* 'I planted the vine; the mulberry, my father. But my grandfather planted the olive tree.' The olive is also easy to grow and not very demanding; it likes dry weather and poor soil. It's a tough plant, and it has an extraordinary ability to come back to life, as Sophocles reminds us: when you cut or burn an olive tree, you can be sure it will soon send out new shoots. From the earliest civilization, the olive tree and olive oil have, for this and other reasons, enjoyed a magical status in lands along the shores of the Mediterranean.

Synonymous with fertility and rebirth, with endurance and resistance to war and the passage of time, a symbol of peace and wealth, the olive was considered a natural fount of strength and purity in various myths and religions, serving medical, sacred and magical needs. Olive oil was charged with so much power that each step of the process of making it

An olive branch, a symbol of peace and harmony.

had a ritual significance. In ancient Egypt the harvest had to be carried out according to specific rules governing the purity of the workers, while only those who anointed their hair, face and feet with oil were worthy to approach the idols. In Greece it was commonly believed that only virgins and chaste men were eligible to cultivate olives, and impure workers were forbidden to take part in the harvest. According to the sixteenth-century Florentine humanist Pier Vettori, Greek men could only harvest the olives if they hadn't made love with a woman the night before.

As might be expected, given that Palestine was very likely one of the places where olive trees were first domesticated, olive oil is hugely important in the pages of the Bible. As a sign of blessing or consecration, a sign of recognition from God to his people, and of their chosen status among other human races, olive oil is a central element in Jewish and Christian culture. Noah, after sending out a crow to determine

Detail of the white dove returning to Noah from *The Flood*, a 12th-century mosaic from the Cathedral of Monreale near Palermo, Italy.

Glass alabastron used for holding oils, 5th–4th century BCE, Phoenicia.

whether the Flood was over and waiting fruitlessly for it to return, sends out a dove which returns to him carrying an olive branch in its beak. The dove and olive branch announce that God has forgiven his people and symbolizes the firm alliance between both of them (Genesis 8:11).

Moreover, olives and olive oil signify the fertility and vitality of the promised land, rich in honey and olive trees (Deuteronomy 8:8), or sometimes they represent gifts that God gives to his people in reward for their obedience and loyalty. Those who obey his laws will produce oil, wine and wheat in abundance, as a sign of wellbeing and happiness; while for those who don't obey, the prophet Joel announces that 'the field is wasted, the land mourneth; for the corn is wasted: the new wine is dried up, the oil languisheth' (Joel 1:10).

But oil is not merely a symbol of peace and prosperity, it is also, and above all, a mark of holiness. From Tutankhamun

Duccio di Buoninsegna, *The Entry of Christ into Jerusalem,* 1308–11, detail from the Maestà in Siena.

to King David, from Ulysses to Patroclus, kings, princes, dignitaries, aristocrats, heroes, athletes and priests in both West and East have used perfumed oil to mark their holiness, their high social standing or their access to the gods. In many religions and in various eras olive oil was the purest, most precious and most eloquent way to exhibit close relations with the divine, to express majesty, permanence and health.

Speaking to Moses, God ordered an ointment, perfumed and rich in spices, 'composed according to the craft of the perfume maker' (Exodus 26). And this was the first in a long series of biblical balms. When Saul is consecrated king, 'Samuel took a vial of oil, and poured it upon his head, and kissed him, and said, Is it not because the Lord hath anointed thee to be captain over his inheritance?' (1 Samuel 10:1)

A generation later, David, from the dynasty of Judah, would be anointed king by Samuel and so on up to Christ, 'the anointed one'. From the Hebrew *mashiach*, meaning 'anointed', comes the word Messiah; in Greek the word is *Christòs*, which generates *Christ*, who in one person combines the three roles of king, priest and prophet.

The entire life of Christ is punctuated by olives and holy oil, as a sign of his holy nature. When he makes his fateful entrance into Jerusalem, Christ is acclaimed by crowds waving olive branches as well as palms. Today, in many Catholic countries, olive branches are distributed in church on Palm Sunday and later brought back home as a sign of peace. In central Italy olive branches were thought to have powers to ward off evil spirits: a branch that had been blessed and was kept in the house, behind the door or above the bed, meant protection against any type of curse or spell. Crosses made of cane or olives branches and a candle were planted on Holy Cross Day to protect wheat fields against fires and thunderstorms; church bells would ring *ad acquaiura* (rapid, repeated tolling) to keep hail away from the fields, while branches of olive trees were burned so that the smoke would appease the storms.

Its fruit being so precious, olive oil has not only long represented this unequivocally sacred and theological dimension, but also has other mysterious meanings that freely marry religion and superstition, medical and cosmetic purposes, as if the olive were a sort of an intermediary between this life and the next, between men and the gods. Before the arrival of Christ, anointment in the Middle East was a sign of prestige and a health measure to prevent and to cure illnesses. In Babylonia the doctor was called *asu*, meaning 'the oil expert'. A few drops of olive oil were poured into a basin full of water and the mixture was used by Babylonian priests to read the future. A similar practice continued into the twentieth century: in southern Italy, until quite recently, women would mix olive oil and water to chase away the evil eye, thus Italians say: *la verità viene sempre a galla*: 'the truth always rises to the surface'. Olive oil turns up in another practice used until recently in central Italy, where women would anoint their breasts with sacred oil from the lamps, or dip their nipples in a jar of oil when breast milk failed to flow.[2]

Cross fashioned from cane with olive branches.

In the Middle Ages holy oil was also used as a cure for the sick and for women possessed by the devil. One of the most popular devotional practices was linked to the tomb of St Nicholas of Myra, in Lycia in today's Turkey. According to Jacobus de Voragine's *Legenda aurea* (*Golden Legend*), a thirteenth-century collection of hagiographies, when the Turks occupied Myra they opened the tomb of St Nicholas and the bones of the saint were found 'floating in oil'. On the lid of the sarcophagus, in fact, are several funnel-shaped holes through which various liquids and perfumed essences were poured into the tomb. This dense and perfumed oily liquid that issued from other holes at the bottom of the tomb was bottled in tiny vials and offered to the faithful as a sacred oil for miraculous healing.

Although olive oil does not seem to have played a great part in ancient Greek cuisine, the olive tree had great symbolic significance there and olive oil was highly prized as a cosmetic. Scented oil was made at least as far back as the third millennium BCE. Lists of different kinds of balsamic oils from the Mycenaean era have been found in Pylos on the Peloponnesus, while at Mycenae itself, archaeologists have unearthed lists of scents – fennel, sesame, cress, mint, sage, rose and juniper – that would have been mixed with oil to make different ointments. Small flasks of precious perfumed oil came to Greece from the Middle East in the eighth century. Homer's heroes draw power, strength and youthfulness from using perfumed oils: Nausicaa kept her bath oil in a golden flask while Achilles anointed Patroclus's body, putting honey and oil on his tomb (*Iliad*, book XLIX). The pre-Socratic philosopher Democritis of Abdera, when asked about the secret to his unusual longevity, used to answer: 'honey inside; olive oil outside'.

Precious balms based on olive oil were used to anoint the bodies of Egyptian Pharaohs, Etruscan aristocrats and Greek

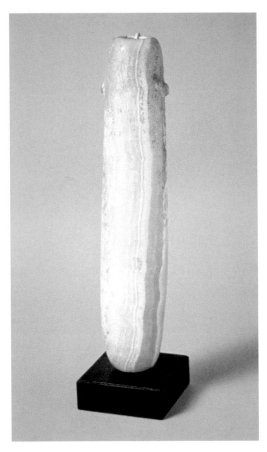

Alabaster unguent jar, 1580–1085 BCE, Egypt.

and Roman athletes preparing themselves for competition. In classical Greece, as the English scholar John Boardman has written,

> it was regular practice for athletes or others who had indulged in energetic work, even women, to rub olive oil on their bodies and then scrape off the mixed oil, dirt and sweat with a scraper called a *strigil* . . . a fine bronze

Bronze strigil, 5th–4th century BCE, from Magna Graecia. Perfumed oil was applied to the body and then a strigil would be used to scrape it off, together with dirt and sweat.

implement so personal a piece of equipment that it formed a regular part of the grave furniture of a man's tomb.[3]

Rubbing the skin with oil served more than aesthetic purposes: in countries as dry as Greece, where the skin easily shrivels and cracks, it was a necessity.

The Romans also made great use of oil for cosmetic purposes as well as in the kitchen; according to Pliny 'there are two liquids especially agreeable to the human body: wine inside, and oil outside'. Innumerable bottles and ampoules in glass, silver, gold, bronze, ivory, ceramic and wood, which went by the names of *lekythoi, alabastron* or *aryballos*, were made to contain the precious liquid. Most of them were small, elongated vases with a tiny handle; elegant ladies would attach them to their wrists like a bracelet and carry them to the bath along with their personal soap. Both were kept in a fine silver casket. In Republican times the Romans tended to condemn these niceties as oriental luxuries, but under the Empire the use of cosmetics exploded. The Roman agricultural expert

Lucius Junius Moderatus Columella wrote that the best oil used to make balsams and perfumes came from the pulp of the most prized olive varieties, of which Licinia olives were among the best, followed by those from Sergia and Colminia. The olives had to be hand-picked before they were completely ripe and crushed with a suspended grindstone so as not to break the stone. The same was done for the 'gleucine oil', an aromatic oil mixed with grape must and various spices, used for everyday ointments and prescribed for those who suffered nervous strain.[4]

Olive oil did not only play a fundamental role in Christian life from birth to death: it was also used to consecrate living and ritual spaces. It brought light to human beings and was therefore considered a direct sign of God's presence among men. And it had to be oil pressed from olives, for this burned with far less smoke than other fats. One of the most ancient and detailed descriptions of an oil lamp is of the golden oil lamp with seven branches always lit in the Second Temple in Jerusalem (described in Exodus 25:31–40). The Temple Menorah is said to have been stolen by the Romans during the siege of Jerusalem in 70 CE and taken back to Rome; it can be seen pictured on the reliefs of the Arch of Titus at the Forum.

Votive lamps also existed in Egypt, although we do not know which of the extant lamps were devoted to the sun-god Ra – lamps in which the oil made from the thousands of olive trees planted by Ramses burned. Among the excavated lamps is a lotus-shaped oil burner in fine alabaster with three arms (possibly an ancestor of the Menorah), found by British archaeologist Howard Carter when he opened Tutan-khamun's tomb in 1922, and today kept in the Cairo Museum.

The Islamic tradition also emphasizes the role of olive oil as a source of light, and considers it basic to that culture. From it, we have inherited the tale of a fabulous oil lamp that, when rubbed, delivers magical results and is able to compensate for Aladdin's miserable life by transforming him into a prince.

The Prophet himself recommended that oil be used not only in cooking but also for body care and to cure over 60 illnesses. Using olive oil was supposed to ward off evil for 40 days. According to scholars of an Islamic holy book, the Sunna, after the Great Flood the olive was the first tree to grow on the emerging land, and so Mohammed called it the blessed tree. To dream of pressing olives and oil was supposed to bring good luck and wealth.[5] One of the most famous verses of the Koran speaks of oil as a symbol of knowledge and light:

> Allah is the light of the heavens and the earth; a likeness of His light is as a niche in which is a lamp, the lamp is in a glass, (and) the glass is as it were a brightly shining star, lit from a blessed olive-tree, neither eastern nor western, the oil whereof almost gives light though fire touch it not – light upon light – Allah guides to His light whom He pleases, and Allah sets forth parables for men, and Allah is Cognizant of all things. (Sura 24)

The medieval Iranian mystic Al-Ghazali (1058–1111), writing of olive oil, the pomegranate, the apple and the quince, said that oil signifies the reasoning intellect because it brings light. Reason – or rather the lack of it – also figures in the parable of the Wise and Foolish Virgins in the gospel of Matthew. Ten virgins have been asked to attend a wedding. While waiting for the bridegroom, they all fall fast asleep, but the oil in their lamps continues to burn. When the bridegroom finally arrives the five Foolish Virgins have run out of oil and have to run to the dealers to try to find some. The bridegroom arrives when they are gone, and the Wise Virgins, who had brought along extra flasks of oil for this eventuality, are able to follow him. But the Foolish Virgins are left behind and miss the wedding feast.

The olive became profoundly rooted in Christian doctrine and Catholic religious iconography in the sixteenth century when Mary was linked with the *oliva speciosa*, a plant in the walled garden, the *hortus conclusus* (which itself symbolized Mary's virginity and protection from sin), along with other plants symbolizing mercy, strength and purity. For reasons that were exquisitely political, the olive began to appear in Renaissance paintings of the Annunciation, as the art historian Cristina Acidini Luchinat has observed.[6] Produced in the fifteenth and sixteenth centuries, these Sienese school paintings depict the Angel Gabriel with a leafy olive branch in hand, symbolizing Siena, rather than the lily that represented the city's great rival, Florence. So peace supplanted purity.

In the patristic and medieval tradition Mary was often worshipped as Notre Dame des Oliviers, Our Lady of the Olives. The *Oliva speciosa* ('fair olive tree', sometimes also *oliva fecunda*, or 'fruitful olive', or *oliva pinguissima*, 'fat, rich olive', or *oliva mitis*, 'meek and mild olive') is widespread in sanctuaries of this title in France, Italy and Spain, signifying true and loving dedication to the Lord, but also symbolizing Mary's strength, power to intercede and mercy. A wooden statue of Notre Dame des Oliviers survived the fire caused by lightning that destroyed the Church of Murat in Cantal, France in 1493. Ever since, the medal of Notre Dame des Oliviers has been said to safeguard those who wear it against lightning, and to protect women who are about to become mothers. The title Our Lady of the Olives may refer to the wood in which the statue was carved, or perhaps alludes to Jesus' suffering at the Mount of Olives, a suffering, according to another interpretation, that is visible in the sombre hue of

Giampaolo Tomassetti, copy by Nicola Barbino (1832–1891),
Madonna dell'olivo ('Madonna of the Olives'), oil on canvas.

the face and body of the statue. The colours of the Virgin, which elsewhere are white and blue, are green at Murat, where the Virgin's mantle reflects the colour of olives. Her feast day is celebrated on the first Sunday in September.

At Christmas and during the olive harvest ritual dishes were served in Provence and Southern Sicily, propitiatory offerings in hopes of a good harvest. Food historian Maguelonne Toussaint-Samat writes that until a few decades ago, at the olive harvest of St Andrew's Day in Provence the trees were beaten with long sticks, traditional songs were sung, and the day ended with a celebration of the olive: an enormous dish of *aioli*, with day labourers, masters and neighbours all seated together under the trees. When the feast was over, people danced the Ouliveto and the Farandole, and sang around the oil presses.[7] Similarly, a dish called *bagna cauda*, bread and vegetables dipped in hot, seasoned oil, is considered a sort of feast in the area between Provence, Liguria and Piedmont.

In Umbria, at the end of the olive harvest, the workers used to make a kind of bough called *la frasca* of laurel, olive and fir branches. It was fixed to the top of a pole, from which various gifts hung. This tree of abundance would then be taken to the houses of the head workers, and they in exchange would offer a meal to everyone.

The ritual use of olive oil during fast days or for propitiatory rites during the olive harvest is rare today. In Egypt Copts still abstain from every kind of animal food (meat, eggs, milk, butter and cheese) during Lent, and they use olive oil for one of their main Lenten dishes, made of vegetables and *dukkah*, a mixture of minced spices that they eat with bread.[8]

In short, the symbolic meanings of the olive and olive oil are many and widespread. Where the Romans arrived, and later where the Church took hold, the olive tree was planted

Olive harvest, southern Italy.

and became essential. The path from the altar and church lamps soon enough reached the table, and oil was used for domestic as well as ritual purposes – and it was one of the most precious items in any household by far. In the words of a popular Sicilian proverb: 'Disgrace if you spill oil on the table; grace, if you spill wine.' The two liquids represent two contrary aspects of life: oil represents measure and balance; wine, excess and lack of moderation. According to Greek mythology, Apollo was born under an olive tree in Delos; thus oil is an Apollonian substance, while wine is Dionysian.

Seen from this perspective, the vine and the olive represent two different styles of life: to consume the 'midnight oil' is considered a mark of diligence and application, while a night spent consuming wine suggests sociability and intemperance.

Olive oil was far too precious to be wasted or thrown away. Its many uses in lighting, medicine, cosmetics and for cooking meant olive oil played an important role in both public and private life until the industrial revolution introduced other kinds of oil and at least until gas came to illuminate our houses. But the powerful symbolic and mythological 'halo' surrounding the olive continues to glow right up to the present – right up to the concept of the 'Mediterranean Diet', which, with its liberal reliance on olive oil, exhibits all the intensity and magic the olive had in antiquity and medieval times.

3
Harvesting, Pressing and Curing

The riper the berry the more greasy and less pleasant the flavour of the oil. The best time for gathering olives, striking a balance between quality and quantity, is when the berries begin to turn dark.

Pliny the Elder, *Natural History*

Olive oil and sesame oil are among the most ancient oils in the Western world and, as we have seen, olive oil was initially used as an unguent, not for food or fuel. Other fats were used for cooking, and animal fat was often used in place of oil. For example, the Roman writer Marcus Portius Cato suggested using lard to make sweet wine cakes and for the doughnut-like *globi encytum*.[1] These were fried in lard and then spread with honey. Even today in Sicily, there are some rather puritanical traditionalists who insist that classical sweets, like *cannoli*, should be fried in lard, not in olive or any other kind of oil, and several other sweets are made with lard instead of butter or olive oil. Elsewhere, where the olive did not grow, other oil seeds were raised. In Egypt, prior to the introduction of the olive, oil was extracted from radish seeds. Pliny wrote that even in his day, people grew radishes in preference to corn because of their high oil yield and the resulting greater profit. Other oil plants were moringa, known since ancient times in Egypt, and the castor oil plant, mostly used for medicine. The oil commonly used in Mesopotamia was made from sesame seeds or almonds.[2]

At first, just a few drops of olive oil squeezed from the tiny black berries of the *oleaster* were sufficient to prepare perfumes, balms and ointments for use in ceremonies. These precious balsams were obtained in a very rudimentary way, by squeezing the olives by hand or underfoot (just as grapes used to be trod upon to make wine) and carefully storing the drops in tiny ceramic jars.

Crushing by hand was a precursor to using a mortar and pestle. Crushing came first, then pressing. Even in the twentieth century, Antonio Carpuso writes, peasants in Morocco and in southern Italy were still crushing the olives in a stone mortar with a big wooden pestle, reducing them to a thick paste and then stuffing the paste into a fabric sleeve.[3] Then, grasping the two ends, they would twist the sleeve so that the oil would 'sweat' out and drip into a vase. To extract all the oil left in the sleeve, hot water was poured over it and it was squeezed again twice or three times. When the process was

Olive press, red granite, Luxor, middle of the 7th century BCE.

Crushing olives with a fragment of ancient column, Beit Jibrin, Palestine, early 20th century

Putting crushed olives into basket containers for pressing.

finished, the oil would float on the water in the vase and could be drained off the top.

The earliest known evidence of the crushing and pressing process has been unearthed in Palestine, and is to be seen at the Museum of the Olive in Haifa. This ensemble of a mortar and a pestle, dating back to some time around the fifth millennium BCE, was possibly the first type of instrument used to crush ripe olives. The olives were first reduced to paste in the mortar; then the paste was enclosed in a crown of olive branches to keep it together, and pressed on large flat stones, piled one on top of the other, to squeeze out the oil. On Crete,

Olive press, Haifa. The weighted beam pressed on discs full of olive paste. Grooves in the stone sent the oil into purpose-built receptacles.

where we know that the olive oil industry was of primary importance from around 2500 BCE, we find more sophisticated technology such as a levered press, in which a beam weighted with heavy stones bore down upon fibre discs containing the olive paste. To extract the oil left in the paste, the olives were drenched with hot water and then pressed again. The resulting liquid was poured into vats and the oil allowed to rise to the top, after which the water was drawn off through a spout at the bottom.

A rudimentary example of the levered press – certainly a revolutionary technology for its time – was excavated at Haifa, where the olives were crushed with huge circular stones; after this the olive paste was stuffed into sacks made

Olive press, Tel Mique-Ekron. The olives were crushed in the central cavity by round stones; side craters held stacks of fibre discs, through which paste was pushed by the pressure exercised by the weighted beams.

of plant fibres, which were piled one upon another. The oil was squeezed out using a beam attached to the wall, on which weights were hung to exert pressure.

A further refinement in the process was discovered a few decades ago not far from Tel Aviv in the enormous olive processing plant containing nearly 100 presses excavated in Tel Mique-Ekron. Here the press was composed of three carved stones: a central one to press and crush the olives, and two lateral ones with a deeper hole in the middle on which to pile, one on top of the other, the large flat discs filled with olive paste. Later on, the crushing was done by a large mill-stone turning in an open tub, into which the olives were tipped whole, and came out as a paste.

The Romans were probably the first to make widespread use of olive oil in cooking and to eat olives in large quantities. They experimented with olive oil to season their polenta, legume soups and bread and they wouldn't cook without it! All aspects of olive cultivation, from curing the olives through oil production, were much improved by the Romans who, as we have seen in chapter One, planted olive trees everywhere they went in their conquest. As far back as Republican Rome, writers such as Cato, in what is today considered a wonderful *summa* of Roman agricultural expertise, the *De agri cultura (On Farming)*, promoted olive plantations because they were less expensive to maintain than vineyards and needed fewer workers to supervise them. This principle, frequently enunci-ated in Roman agricultural treatises, was deeply rooted in the minds of Roman gentleman farmers from Republican times right up through the Empire and its eventual collapse. This certainly explains why the Romans made great technical advances in oil production, inventing techniques that were used until modern times. The grindstone called *mole olearia* was the most basic; it was made of a round base fixed on the

Crushing olives, Palestine, 1903.

floor with a cylindrical grindstone that turned around an axle, crushing and squeezing the olives.

Depending on how wealthy the owner of the press was, writes Maguelonne Toussaint-Samat, the press was worked by slaves, by a mule or donkey – or even by the wife of the owner![4]

The next step was the invention of the *trapetum*, a large carved stone with a central pivot around which two stone hemispheres rotated. Once the olives were crushed, the oil was extracted by a press, either a screw press or a simple wooden beam on which weights were hung.

The *trapetum* crushed the olives against the sides of the mortar, rather than against the base. It was expensive and hard to build, because it was necessary to calculate the exact distance between the millstone and the mortar, so it was used only on large estates, while in small villages they continued to use the grindstone on a stone mortar with a truncated conic shape, an easier and cheaper method.

The instructions given by all the Roman agrarian experts about when to pick the olives and how to extract the oil were so detailed that we can easily follow them today. All agreed

Amphora with an olive-gathering scene. A young man shakes down the olives. Two bearded figures, one on each side, with purple drapery round the loins, are beating the trees with long sticks; the one on the right wears a *pilos*. At the foot of the tree is a nude youth kneeling to the right, gathering up the olives into a basket as they fall, 520 BC.

that the harvest must be done with great care, and that the olives had to be picked by hand without using sticks to knock them off the branches, ideally before the olives fell to the ground. The best moment for the harvest was early November, when a few olives had just started to turn brown but most were still nice and green. The Romans called the oil extracted from these olives, which have just started changing colour but are not yet ripe, *Oleum viride*, for its wonderful greenish-gold colour. From the first pressing of those olives one obtained top-quality oil; the two subsequent pressings give second quality, and then ordinary oil.

The ancient writers also made it clear that olive oil turned bad very quickly, and it was recommended that a store of olives be kept handy so that oil needed for the table could be produced immediately before use. Be aware, Cato wrote, that as soon as you collect them, you have to process the oil from the olives before they spoil . . . Think of the rains which fall every year and make the berries drop to the ground. If you collect them early and are prepared to stock them you won't have any damage and the oil will turn out to be green, and the best. If you leave them on the ground too long or on a table, the olives will start to go rancid and the olive oil will stink . . .[5]

Pliny the Elder set down a scale of oil quality which is still valid. He explained that the same olive could produce different types of oil. When the olive was still green and unripe, you obtained the best, most exquisite oil, called *Oleum ex albis ulivis*, very similar to the *Oleum viride* mentioned above. The riper the olive, the denser the oil and the less agreeable it tasted. But even then there were important differences in oil quality depending on whether maturation took place in the crusher or on the tree, and whether the tree had been irrigated or not. The other oils were cheaper types, such as *Oleum maturum* from black ripe olives, which was decidedly less good quality compared to the others; *Oleum caducum*, made from olives that had fallen on the ground and were very ripe; and *Oleum cibarium*, the worst of all, made of rancid olives and consumed by slaves or used for other purposes, such as lighting.[6]

In medieval Italy local authorities would establish the date of the olive harvest, but most often it began on St Martin's Day, 11 November, and was usually completed before Christmas. Afterwards, the men made their last pass, picking up the remaining olives on the ground or those left on the trees. In southern Italy, in Latium and in Liguria, the olives were knocked off the trees with sticks and the berries collected on large cotton sheets spread on the ground. Even today in

Olives are collected in nets on the ground.

Olive harvest, Sicily.

Tuscany you can find farmers collecting the olives the way Marcus Terentius Varro advised: picking them by hand, right up to the top of the tree, without using sticks as the slaves used to do because they damaged the berry and broke the fine branches, exposing the tree to frost damage the following winter. In Tuscany, those hand-picked olives are placed in little baskets hanging from the farmer's arm.[7] As Pliny tells it, some time always passed between the harvest and the crushing of the olives, and during this time the olives could rest on wooden tables so long as they were undamaged. But if they had been damaged by insects or were even just bruised, they would soon go rancid and produce a bad oil. Today olives are held for no more than 48 hours after the harvest.

Although the process of making olive oil is very ancient, the notion of eating this bitter berry and the means to cure it seem to have come later and with greater difficulty. The Bible cites oil and its sacred uses far more often than it mentions olives. And olives rarely appear in classical or medieval recipe books. This doesn't necessarily mean that people didn't eat them, however. It is probable that olives were too humble for aristocratic tables (the only source of written recipes up until modern times) and they were most likely too obvious – and too poor – a food to mention in writing. But dried, brined or salted, they were probably a common food for peasants and workers. Their high fat content (and calorific value) and their omnipresence suggests they would certainly have been eaten all around the Mediterranean. Nourishing and easy to carry, to prepare and to store, olives – more than any other fruit, once people learned how to cure them – became a pillar of the rustic diet in Spain, Italy and Greece, as they still are today. What could be more delicious than a bowl of green or black olives, a loaf of bread, some cheese and a good bottle of wine?

Cured olives were left in the Pharaoh's tomb to provide food for the afterlife, despite the fact that the Egyptians didn't make much use of olives or olive oil in their diet. The Phoenicians may have known that olives that had spontaneously fallen from the tree and lain on the ground were good to eat; when olives matured that way they lost much of their bitterness. Homer referred in several places to the olive berry: pickled, brined and highly seasoned. We know that the Etruscans traded oil extensively, probably mostly for cosmetic use. But in an Etruscan tomb in Cerveteri, archaeologists found olive stones which had been left as an offering for the dead, while olives preserved in brine were discovered inside Etruscan amphorae found on a sunken ship near the island of Giglio, and dated to around the sixth century BCE.

Archestratus, a comic poet and classical Greek food expert, mentions ripe black olives in his recipes only once. But he always used olive oil to cook, and he urged a very simple cuisine seasoned with salt and oil, in preference to the elaborate style of cooking that was popular in Greek Sicily, which he considered far too rich.[8]

While most olives are cultivated to produce oil, some varieties are selected to be cured in lye, brine or dry salt.

Cato mentions olives and bread as being staples in the diet of the peasants and labourers.[9] His workers' rations consisted of bread, wine, salt and olives. Rather miserly, he recommended they be given the windfall olives and mature fruit with a high oil yield, even though they were often rotten. The olives were to be distributed sparingly and, when used up, should be replaced by pickled fish and vinegar. Each man was allowed a pint of the oil each month. But nothing was wasted, and so a sort of oil cake, made from olive paste left over from the last pressing, called *sampsa*, was given to the poorest, or sold as a snack in the markets, flavoured with salt, cumin,

Olive focaccia, a traditional Italian bread that uses olive oil and the olives themselves. For recipe, see p. 101.

anise, fennel and olive oil. Meanwhile the best-preserved olives appeared mostly on the tables of the wealthier classes.

Right up until the 1970s workers on large estates in Sicily had the right to receive one litre of olive oil per month; their daily diet (at noon) consisted of a one-kilogram loaf of bread, one litre of wine, 100 grams of cheese (usually ricotta) and a handful of olives. In the evening, they got 250 grams of pasta cooked with wild greens. This was considered a desirable ration, since most farm labourers didn't have pasta or bread as often as they wanted.

The Romans cured olives in many different ways and at different stages of ripeness. Just as the Roman guidelines for making oil are the first we know of, so they also set down the first rules on record for curing olives, rules still followed today. Green olives were to be preserved in salt brine, or they were first crushed and then repeatedly washed in water, and

Olives in brine with wild fennel.

finally seasoned in brine flavoured with vinegar, fennel and other spices. Sometimes they were pressed and kept in jars with layers of fennel and mastic at the top and bottom, filled with brine, must, vinegar, even occasionally honey. The half-ripe berries were cured in olive oil, while the ripe ones were and still are sprinkled with salt, left for five days and then dried in the sun. Pitted ripe black olives were cured in jars with oil, coriander, cumin, fennel, rue and mint; this was known as oil salad and was eaten with cheese. Cato mentions a special dish known as *epityrum* which was considered to have been a Sicilian invention: it consisted of stoned green, black and mottled olives chopped and mixed with oil, vinegar, coriander, cumin, fennel, rue and mint, placed in an earthenware dish and covered with oil to serve.

As continues to be the case today, olives were not considered a proper meal in antiquity, but were eaten as a side dish or hors d'oeuvre with bread, cheese and onions. This was true in ancient Greece and at the Roman banquet, which usually started with a *gustatio o promulsis*, like the modern antipasto, made of ripe black olives, green olives in brine, salad, lightly poached wild asparagus and wine.[10] Today olives are offered as an antipasto on Italian tables in much the same way. In Tunisia, one of the main African producers of olive oil under the Roman Empire, in the Maghreb and north-west Africa today, olives are an important ingredient in dishes like *tagine*, a stew cooked in a special pot and described as 'smothered in olives'.[11] Strangely enough, however, olive oil is not used in Moroccan or North African cuisine, except in Tunisia, while in Italy, Greece, Spain and Portugal it is universal.

After the Roman Empire declined, when northern invaders brought a taste for lard, pork fat became a staple in the everyday European diet. The techniques for producing oil for culinary use and for curing olives were lost and most

Roasted olives with orange zest, an antipasto. For recipe, see p. 91.

Green olive salad, a Sicilian antipasto. For recipe, see p. 90.

of the oil produced was used to make soap or for industrial purposes. The body of knowledge accumulated by the Romans was forgotten for at least eleven centuries. In 1574 Pier Vettori, an erudite Tuscan, once again established the precepts for making good oil, and it began to be produced in Provence and Tuscany. But high-quality oil was now a luxury product too expensive for everyday use by the peasantry.

Elsewhere in Italy, especially Sicily, the techniques for producing good oil were utterly unknown. Oil was pressed from olives harvested on the ground, contrary to the ancient Roman practice. It was stored in smelly goatskin bags, with the inevitable consequences! It was believed that olives that had been stored for a while gave the most oil, and so, after the harvest, the olives were left to pile up and ferment in a corner of the house, sprinkled with salt, while they awaited their turn at the press. In Sicily, to determine whether the olives were ready, the farmer plunged his arm into the putrefying mess; if the arm came out white and oiled, they were ready to press, but if the arm came out red, like the olive pulp, that meant they were still raw. Foreign travellers rightly avoided using this oil to dress their salads when they went south of Naples, given the powerful and usually rancid flavour it had.[12] Under the circumstances, it should come as no surprise that Martin Luther, in his reforming zeal, preached against the olive oil imposed by the Church during fasting: beyond any questions of morality, there was also a problem of taste, for much of the oil in circulation was of very poor quality.

In any case, sixteenth-century Europe was soon divided in two parties: the butter-users and those who much preferred olive oil. And the situation hasn't changed much since then.

It was not merely a question of religious belief, according to French food historian Jean-Louis Flandrin,[13] but also an issue of taste: northerners simply disliked olive oil (and here,

Pieter Claesz., *Still-life,* early 17th century, oil on canvas.

it would be interesting to know what quality of oil was exported to those countries) and dreamed of an oil that would be colourless and tasteless, bland and without any olive scent. So the path to industrial olive oil production was opened.

At the time, obtaining both good butter and good olive oil was a matter of price; both were very expensive, synonymous with luxury and high social rank. For the upper class, the choice was not merely based on geography – north or south – it was also a question of palate. High social status or particular local habits sometimes led people to break the rules; thus aristocrats in France or England might use olive oil while their countrymen were butter-eaters. Countess Mahaut, a fifteenth-century French aristocrat from Artois, regularly used olive oil. In English recipe books of the same period, the dishes made with olive oil are mostly those enjoyed by the ranks of the aristocracy. And vice versa: a Neapolitan recipe book of the fifteenth century prescribes butter more often than lard and just as often as olive oil, and the local ravioli stuffed with local cheese are fried in butter! Thus the famous opposition between fats – butter versus olive oil – is not just a matter of north and south, but also a matter of social distinctions.

Something similar is going on in the gorgeous Dutch still-lifes of the sixteenth century, where a lavish and bountiful nature includes an abundance of exotic ingredients – often including a tray or a bowl filled with olives. In those times and in that place far to the north, those olives certainly represented peace and prosperity, just as they do in the Bible, but they were also a marker of distinction, of wealth, of exceptional luxury. Those same olives that in Cato's time were doled out as food to the workers were now treasured in an expensive Chinese bowl on the Flemish table!

4
The Olive Meets the New World

The olive's noblest function is, of course, to keep a lemon twist
out of your Martini ...

L. R. Shannon

My wife says Ambersons don't make lettuce salad the way
other people do; they don't chop it up with sugar and
vinegar at all. They pour olive oil on it with their vinegar
and they have it separate – not along with the rest of the
meal. And they eat these olives, too: green things they are,
something like a hard plum, but a friend of mine told me
they tasted a good deal like bad hickory-nuts. My wife
says she is going to buy some; you got to eat nine and
then you get to like 'em, she says. Well, I wouldn't eat nine
bad hickory-nuts to get to like them, and I'm going to let
these olives alone. Kind of a woman's dish anyway, I
suspect but most everybody will be making a stagger to
worm through nine of 'em, now Ambersons brought
'em to town. Yes, sir, the rest'll eat 'em, whether they get
sick or not!

In his 1918 novel *The Magnificent Ambersons* Booth Tarkington
casts a deliciously ironic glance at the culinary habits of the

new American bourgeoisie in the early years of the twentieth century. In those days – before the taste for French cuisine and long before the Mediterranean diet was ever heard of – the New World palate was still largely virgin. Our narrator seems to know nothing of the lands where olives are grown, he finds the idea of eating them repellent, and he doesn't really approve of his patrician neighbours, the 'magnificent' Ambersons, who are so outrageously cosmopolitan as to eat their salad as a side dish, dressed not with sickly sweet sauces but merely with olive oil and vinegar. You couldn't get much further from the 'Flapper Salad' popular in the 1920s, made of lettuce, maraschino cherries, mayonnaise, pears, cheese and artificial colourings. Middle-class Americans didn't know or care about the long history of the olive in the Mediterranean and the Middle East – and few were yet aware that olives were becoming the signature garnish for the Martini, one of the most fashionable cocktails of the Roaring Twenties.

It would be a while yet before olives and olive oil became familiar to Americans and part of their daily diet. Although olive oil had for a long time been produced in California, it never really found a us market. The only potential consumers were Italian-Americans, and they preferred to import their oil from Italy. The only olives that caught on in America were the little green ones in Martinis and the big, ripe black California olives, so very unlike pungent Italian or Spanish olives. With their 'gentle' – in other words, bland – flavour, California olives caught on quickly in the United States and, right up to the 1980s, were the only ones to be found in many places.

And yet the olive tree was one of the very first Old World plants to be transplanted to the Americas. The first olive trees in the New World arrived in Hispaniola and Cuba as early as 1520, sent from Olivares in the Aljarafe region near Seville.

Ancient olive tree cared for by Franciscan monks at the Garden of Gerusalem, American colony, Jerusalem, 1900–10.

When the Spanish conquistadors reached Peru in 1560, they also brought olive cuttings. But it was thanks to the patient agricultural skills of Franciscan, Jesuit and Dominican missionaries that olives, along with many other European fruits, were widely cultivated in South America, and then in Mexico, finally reaching Alta California in the late 1700s. The olives were planted by Franciscan friars who strayed north from San

Blas in Mexico and who later founded the San Diego de Alcalà Mission in what is today San Diego, in 1769. The friars planted the olive trees mainly for their own use: to provide the oil they used for cooking and lighting, for making soaps, to prepare wool for spinning and to lubricate machinery.

The missionaries maintained their olive groves until Mexico's emancipation from the Spanish crown in 1822, when the new Mexican government took possession of all Spanish public lands in California. Eleven years later, in 1833, Mexico secularized the missions, seizing the land from the church and attaching it to the colony of California. When the Franciscans left the missions and abandoned their fields and orchards, there was no one to tend them, and the olive groves languished. Nevertheless, a few trees survived at the San Jose mission and in San Diego, while the oldest ones, dating back to 1805, were still alive at the Santa Clara mission in 1996, as recalled by Judith M. Taylor.[1]

These scanty but tenacious shoots of Old World culture and of the olive's several thousand-year-old history were the germ of a new direction for the olive. This new chapter in its story takes place not in little orchards or family olive groves but on a global scale, in vast, single-crop tracts of olive trees on nearly every continent, using intensive agriculture and the most sophisticated technology.

Between 1850 and 1900 olive growers in California had begun to improve their product. Cultivars were imported from Mediterranean countries and by the end of the century California growers had mastered the art of making good olive oil. Production increased notably. But for various reasons, olive oil produced in America did not find much of a domestic market. The great majority of the rapidly expanding US population had never even tasted olives and had only a marginal taste for olive oil. The same was true in Britain: during the eighteenth and nineteenth centuries, the olive oil exported from southern Italy to Great Britain was largely used to grease factory machinery, while a small quantity was used, grudgingly, as medicine. As the old English saying 'brown as olive oil' suggests, most people in Britain had never even seen good olive oil, let alone tasted it. Up until the 1970s pharmacies were the only place in Britain where one could find olive oil. It was stocked as a laxative.

In the US only the Hispanic population ate olives; they alone knew how to cure them and how to cook with olive oil. In California they most probably harvested olives from the trees abandoned at the missions, while later, when Italian immigrants arrived en masse to the US in the second half of the nineteenth century, they bought and used olive oil liberally, but not, as we have seen, the oil produced in California. Nearly 80 per cent of the immigrants who settled in California came from regions where olives had been cultivated for centuries: Lucca in Tuscany, and Sicily. They understood the value of California's olive groves and possessed the skills to cultivate and prune the trees.

Yet it was precisely the Italians of this mass immigration who consistently bought imported Italian olive oil right up until the 1910s. The early Italian-American community remained astonishingly faithful to the original Italian product and in general to those foods considered key elements of their cultural identity. Between 1898 and 1910 the consumption of imported olive oil increased three-fold. Italian-American families were willing to do without heat and drastically reduce their diets, but they did not sacrifice their olive oil, pasta and wine,[2] as Mario Puzo writes:

> During the Great Depression of the 1930s, though we were the poorest of the poor, I never remember not

dining well. Many years later as a guest of a millionaire's club, I realized that our poor family on home relief ate better than some of the richest people of America. My mother would never dream of using anything but the finest imported olive oil, the best Italian cheeses . . . [3]

Olive oil consumption by Italians abroad continued to grow up to 1929. Oil had become one of the leading Italian imports in the US. Nevertheless, after the First World War the pattern of exports changed radically. Oil was now produced in the New World and a new class of consumers was born. The Great Depression coincided with the meteorological 'big chill' of 1929, a freeze that killed more than half the olive trees in Italy. The country's overall production of oil fell by 50 per cent, and the US market for Italian oil collapsed. At the same time, the mass Italian immigration to the US fell to a trickle with the application of tough new immigration laws. Suddenly, demand for high-quality Italian oil fell off sharply. Italy could not provide it and Italian-Americans had stopped consuming it. The war on the one hand and the growth of Italian-American communities on the other (by now most such 'Italians' were born in America) created the conditions for Italian-Americans to produce what they needed for their diet in the New World. Second-generation Italian-Americans tended to know less than their parents about quality olive oil. And often they shared the American taste for the bland, mass-produced flavour of inexpensive cottonseed oil. Their shops would no longer sell homemade cans of oil fresh in from Sicily and smudged with dirt.[4]

In Brooklyn, people now spoke *broccolino*, a mixture of Sicilian, Neapolitan and New York English. They wanted to buy tins of olive oil and other products that conjured up the idealized memory they had of Italy – and the country they dreamed of was a concentrated blend of sun, food and beauty. It was that ideal they wanted to see on a label; they were not so interested in where the food had been grown or when it was harvested or packed. A can of oil, a package of pasta: they were pretexts to dream and indulge in a powerful nostalgia. San Remo brand, Italian Product, packed in Italy; Marca Sole Mio, impaccato in Italia per C. Torrielli, Boston, Mass.; Orlando Brand, per la mensa siciliana, pure virgin olive oil, packed in Italy: such were the brands Italians bought.[5] High-quality olive oil became scarce and many unscrupulous dealers sold greasy, insipid, adulterated oil as pure 'extra-virgin' olive oil. A new method of refining cottonseed oil developed in the United States allowed olive oil to be cut with cottonseed oil to get more profit out of it.

Olives grown and canned in America were another story. When, at the beginning of the twentieth century, American oil producers ceded the market to Italian imports, it was not just a question of palate, but of profits. Olive oil produced in the US was far more expensive than that imported from Italy,[6] largely because of higher labour costs. Italy's sharecrop labour force meant that even with the cost of transportation, importers could undercut the domestic product. The industry in the US thus shifted to canning olives.

Huge plantations for the canning industry grew up in the Central Valley. But in Sonoma and Napa, great trees dating back to the state's early history were dug out to plant vines or sent south to decorate parking lots around Los Angeles. And then late in the 1980s, when a growing number of Americans began to realize what olive oil could do for them, Californians again noticed the trees that remained.[7]

The queen of canned olives was a German-born American named Freda Ehmann, the woman who first understood how to package the fruits of the olive tree and how to sell

Harvesting olives in California in the early 20th century.

the sharp, sour, bitter olive to Americans. With the help of the dean of the Agriculture School at the University of California at Berkeley, Ehmann learned how to cure olives so as to reduce what might be called their 'ethnic' taste, so they no longer tasted piquant like Spanish olives but had a mild flavour that pleased a diffident American palate. Olives had traditionally been packed in large casks in brine, but Ehmann soon had the idea of packaging them in small quantities, so they were easy to store and transport.

Born in Germany in 1839, the daughter of a Lutheran minister, her mother a descendent of Huguenot exiles, Freda Ehmann had moved to the United States as a girl. At the age of 18 she had married a fellow German immigrant and medical doctor, Ernst Cornelius Ehmann, and settled in Quincy, Illinois, to be a wife and mother. When Dr Cornelius died prematurely, she moved to California with her daughter, Emma, to join her son, who had a business venture there. In 1897 she lost the money she had invested in her son's business.

Freda Ehmann testing her cured black olives.

Penniless and middle-aged, Freda Ehmann was not a woman to waste time in self-pity. She started pickling the olives from the family's only asset, a 20-acre orchard, on her daughter's back porch in Oakland. Initially the olives were packed in barrels, then in glass jars, and finally in tin cans. The Ehmann Olive Company quickly became a success, and not only in gourmet circles. By 1905 Ehmann olives were the olive of choice in the US, selling to fancy hotels and famous restaurants nationwide.[8]

Unfortunately Ehmann's personal success story did not have a happy ending. In 1919 improperly processed olives caused the deaths from botulism of 35 people in the East and Midwest. Ehmann's largest canned olive factory went bust. But she lived on until 1932, when at the age of 93 she still lived by a firm set of rules: no alcohol in the house, and no green olives.[9]

Ehmann olives were of course the black 'California ripe' variety. Her lye-cure recipe produced a very mild-tasting olive, similar to the black California olives still found in cans on grocery shelves today. After the botulism episode consumers were wary of canned olives for several years. But confidence in canning methods was restored, and when in the 1920s the Martini with its green olive became *the* Jazz Era drink of choice, and the black ripe olive became a staple of the 'relish tray', olives were absolved. Americans still didn't consume much olive oil, although they sometimes used it to season their salads, but from now on they would consider it a cocktail hour must to have a can of olives in the house. Today, the table olive canning industry absorbs almost 90 per cent of California olive production, and California is responsible for some 6.7 per cent of the world's table olives.

In Italy the olive landscape has changed utterly since the Second World War. The small farms and *mezzadria*, or share-cropping labour force, have disappeared, and along with them

John Singer Sargent, *The Olive Grove*, 1910, oil on canvas.

the mixed crops – vines, olive trees, almonds, peaches, figs and so on – associated with smallholdings. Italy would continue to be the world leader in olive oil production until 1985, when a new freeze would destroy many prime olive groves in central Italy. New orchards planted after the 1985 freeze mean that the time-honoured Italian countryside now looks different. Beginning in 1986, Europe as a whole, not Italy, became the primary exporter, as Spain, Portugal and Greece stepped in to fill the gap. Italy, which up until the mid-1980s was responsible for 34 per cent of world production, now produces just 14 per cent, after Spain, the world's largest producer.

Even more importantly, today – more than 5,000 years into the history of that spiny little bush that became the olive tree – this tasty, oily fruit is no longer an exclusively a Mediterranean affair. The olive and its oil have long sailed past the straits of Gibraltar and reached the Americas, Australia and New Zealand. The sixth millennium has begun.

5
Good Fat and Bad Fat:
The Mediterranean Diet

'Waiter, Extra Olive Oil Please, I Have a Headache'
Robert Lee Hotz, *Los Angeles Times,* 1 September 2005

This virgin and extra virgin is to confuse. A woman
is a virgin or she is not. How can she be extra virgin?
What matters is taste.
Mort Rosenblum, *Olives: The Life and Lore of a Noble Fruit*

In conclusion, allow me to touch on the theme of the Mediterranean Diet, and the near-universal belief today that
healthy eating is linked to a generous use of olive oil in the
kitchen – never mind centuries of Escoffier, Julia Child or
the rigid dietary rules of early twentieth-century America,
when nutritionists believed that immigrant food, including
of course pasta and olive oil, 'led to the consumption of
alcohol, caused overexcitement of the nervous system, and
was indigestible'.[1]

Behind this new passion stands a paradox: there is in
fact no particular, precise place where this Mediterranean
Diet resides. Reams of scientific and gastronomic literature
haven't proved there is any such thing as a Mediterranean
cultural identity but meanwhile scientists, chefs, nutritionists,

food manufacturers and government health advisers have all determined that olive oil is the staple of a correct diet, the so-called Mediterranean Diet. In fact, according to many scholars, it is nearly impossible to find a common link among the various countries that surround the Mediterranean Sea, least of all on culinary grounds. A few point to a shared sense of honour and chastity among women living on the Mediterranean coast, others to some shared social, political or ecological conditions,[2] but the Italian historian Piero Camporesi warned, only half in jest, against this sort of culinary 'Mediterranean infatuation'. According to Camporesi, probably the only thing that could be said to link together the countries that are considered part of the Mediterranean ensemble might be a stew: a thick stew made of meat and vegetables, like what the French call *pot au feu*, the Spanish *olla potrida*, and the Piedmontese *casseula* – perhaps cooked in olive oil. Yet this is a common ingredient for only a few of the so-called Mediterranean countries since most of the Islamic countries prefer to cook with some sort of animal fat, do not drink wine and prefer rice to pasta![3]

The Mediterranean region.

The Mediterranean Diet pyramid.

Paradoxically, too, it is difficult to imagine preferring the 'poor' dietary model of the Mediterranean Diet except in prosperous societies where economic well-being has long been taken for granted. Not by chance, in the regions from which the model of the Mediterranean Diet were drawn – Greece, southern Italy and Spain – that very diet is least popular today. Meat, animal fat and fast food are now symbols of abundance and well-being that were unthinkable for these populations as recently as thirty years ago.

Nevertheless, the Mediterranean Diet and the liberal use of extra virgin olive oil has become an article of faith today for many restaurants and dietary experts. Perhaps for the first time since antiquity, an alliance in the name of olive oil has been made between food producers and experts. How did this come about? Might there be more than just health reasons behind this new alliance?

It was just after the Second World War that experts began to study diets alternative to that popular in the United States. The war had brought a forcible change in habits and it was time for new ideas. Several research organizations began to compare different Western diets: in 1947 the Rockefeller Foundation conducted an epidemiological survey of 765 families in Crete to determine the consequences of food habits. Dr Ancel Keys carried out medical research in Nicotera (Calabria),

Detail of *Neptune and the Four Seasons*, mid-2nd century, mosaic.

Heraklion and Castelli. From those studies came evidence that a diet based on wheat (bread and pasta), unsaturated fat, such as olive oil, as opposed to animal fat, and fresh vegetables and fruits, helped to prevent coronary heart disease. In 1959 Ancel and Margaret Keys wrote the recipe book *Eat Well and Stay Well*, in which they condensed different cuisines from many of the countries belonging to the Mediterranean area, and gave a practical structure to this model that was both dietary and culinary. In many ways this was a great revolution, considering that French cuisine had reigned without any competition since the eighteenth century. *Eat Well and Stay Well* had a big impact in the US and, from there, echoed back to Europe, where the book was translated into Italian in 1962.

Over the next 40 years, the Keys's research would have a profound impact not only in the medical sphere but also in the culinary arena, and would encourage Americans to want to eat a healthier, more balanced diet based on a single type of vegetable fat: olive oil.

Other studies, such as Keys's *Seven Countries: A Multivariate Analysis of Death and Coronary Heart Disease* (1980), reinforced the concept of 'good eating' and the so-called Mediterranean Diet. When the population of Greece was found to have a lower rate of heart disease than the rest of world, the data on diet in the 1948 Rockefeller Foundation report was taken as an explanation, and the presence of 'good' fat, olive oil, in the Greek diet was portrayed as the key element of what became known as the Mediterranean Diet.[4]

In the 1970s and '80s an unusual alliance between science and gastronomy supported the view that an olive oil-based cuisine would bring great health benefits to the individual, and many publications trumpeted the Mediterranean diet. Giorgio De Luca was part of that generation of Italian-Americans who as children in the 1950s were ashamed to go to school with a

Caponata, Sicilian aubergine salad. For recipe, see pp. 91–2.

sandwich filled with the Sicilian aubergine salad *caponata*. In the 1980s, with his partners Joel Dean and Jack Ceglic in the Manhattan food emporium Dean & De Luca, he would be one of the proudest proponents of a new style of life in which balsamic vinegar, sun-dried tomatoes and extra virgin olive oil, three ingredients that came to symbolize a whole way of life, were essential.[5]

In the 1990s the US organization Oldways began promoting the 'traditional Mediterranean diet', which they defined as the dietary habits found, until recent times, in olive-producing areas surrounding the Mediterranean Sea. The Oldways diet is based on abundant plant foods including fresh fruits and vegetables, with olive oil for fat and moderate use of dairy products and fish or poultry. Such eating habits, research has increasingly suggested, are strongly connected with coronary health and a lower rate of other diseases. Olive oil is not only a healthy source of fat, it also contains a high concentration of antioxidants – chlorophyll, carotenoids, and polyphenolic compounds – that help scour away free radicals and preserve the vitamin E in the oil.

The consumption of olive oil in the United States rose from 64 million lb (29 million kilos) in 1982, to 250 million in 1994.[6] In the UK 2006 was the first year that olive sales surpassed that of other vegetable oils since, as market analyst Claire Birks comments, 'the popularity of olive oil has not only been helped by its aspirational value, but also by its association with Mediterranean cooking and the health claims linked with this way of life'.[7]

That is a long way from the laxative section on the chemist's shelf! Nevertheless, one has to wonder: is it only for health reasons that olive oil has supplanted butter – that French cuisine has been discarded in favour of the Mediterranean Diet? Once, dietary experts advised us to limit the amount of fat we eat; today, fats are divided between 'bad' (animal) and 'good' (vegetable).[8] The health benefits of the olive may be undeniable, but I cannot help thinking that the preference for olive oil and 'Mediterranean' habits of eating conceals a deeper demand, a deeper desire.

Olive oil is not merely a type of fat; it stands for an entire alternative way of life. More than a mere ingredient, the olive offers a complete system of values, in which the emphasis is placed on how the oil is extracted by natural and ancient methods that haven't changed since antiquity. The artisanal nature of oil pressing, even though assisted by very modern technologies, makes olive oil the epitome of the 'un-processed',

Luca della Robbia, 'November', *The Labours of the Month*, 1450–56, blue, white and yellow in tin-glazed terracotta.

Harvesting olives in southern Italy.

Vincent van Gogh, *Women Picking Olives*, 1889–90, oil on canvas.

the symbol of an untouched nature, of an anti-industrial world in which 'poor' methods and 'poor' food are preferable to the rich.

Olive oil somehow manages to link us to a very ancient past, the 'pure' past of the Greeks and the Romans, of Homer and Virgil, leaping, entirely anachronistically, over centuries and centuries of modern life, revolutions, bourgeois palates and aristocratic cuisines drenched in butter. To prefer olive oil over butter is, one cannot but feel, like preferring mythology over history; it's a search for a mythic time in some mythic place uncontaminated by the compromises of life in the here and now.

Recipes

Cured olives

The taste of olives depends on when you choose to harvest them. There are three basic ways to cure olives: a dry salt cure for black olives, a lye cure and a brine cure for green olives. The first recipes for salt or brine curing, still much the same as are used today in southern Italy, were recorded by the ancient Roman agricultural expert Lucius Junius Moderatus Columella in his treatise *De re rustica (XII)*.

Curing Green Olives
—from Columella, *De re rustica*

Harvest the olives green before they are completely mature, beat them with a sharp cane and immerse them in hot water, to release their bitterness. After you have drained and dried them, put them in amphorae along with leeks, rue, *apio tenero* (a plant similar to celery) and mint, all finely chopped. Last, pour over them wine seasoned with spices and honey. (*Apium graveolens* is a plant species in the family Apiaceae, known as celery.)

Curing Black Olives
—from Columella, *De re rustica*

Place the black olives, as yet unripe, in wicker baskets, cover them with salt and leave them under the hot September sun for 30–40 days to allow them to sweat. After the natural warmth has dried them off, conserve them in boiled wine must or vinegar mixed with honey, and cover with a layer of fennel mixed with lentiscus.

To Dry Cure the Tiny, Black French Nyons Olives
—This is a modern recipe suggested by Lynn Alley in *Lost Arts*

Mix the olives with their own weight in non-iodized table salt, pickling salt or rock salt. Pour them evenly into a pillowcase and cover them completely with more salt. Put them somewhere so that any juice that dips from them will not stain. Stir or mix them well once a week for four weeks (or until they lose their bitterness). When they are no longer bitter, rinse them carefully and allow them to dry overnight. Then pack them in oil until you are ready to consume them.

To Brine-cure Green Olives
—from Alley, *Lost Arts*

Some people crack the green olives before putting them in brine. Otherwise, you simply place your clean green olives in cold water and change the water each day for ten days. At the end of the ten-day period, you can make a more permanent brine solution in which to continue the process. Add 1 cup of non-iodized salt to each gallon of water. The water should have enough salt to float a raw egg. Use enough of this brine to cover the olives. Change the solution weekly for four weeks. At the end of four weeks transfer the olives to a weaker brine solution until you are ready to use them. This solution should contain ½ cup of non-iodized salt to each gallon of water.

The olives may take up to two or three months to develop their flavour.

Syrian Recipe for Curing Olives
—collected by Charles Perry, expert scholar on the
cuisines of the world, from *The Feast of the Olive*
by Maggie Blyth Klein

Take olives from Palmyra (black for preference) remove the pits and mix with cardamom and ground walnuts. Sprinkle with coriander, toasted walnuts and salted lemon, knead together and put in a jar.

Iraqi Recipe for Curing Olives
—Charles Perry, from *The Feast of the Olive*

Take ripe or green olives (black are better) and crush and salt them. Turn them over every day until their bitterness disappears, then put them on a tray of woven sticks for a day and a night until dry. Pound garlic and dry thyme with an equal weight of walnuts. Put the mixture on a low fire, and put the tray of olives on the same stone in an oven, close the door, and leave a whole day. Stir several times so that the aromas circulate. Take out and season with sesame oil, crushed walnuts, toasted sesame seeds, garlic and thyme.

Bruschetta

Olive oil is essential to one of the most renowned dishes in the world: *bruschetta*. The simplest of dishes, it is, when made with the best ingredients, one of the best. You will find a version of *bruschetta* everywhere around the Mediterranean where olive trees are grown. In Nice they call it *brissa*, in Tuscany, *fettunta*, but the ingredients are virtually identical everywhere: slices of a large loaf of Italian country-style bread, garlic and fresh olive oil. In southern Italy, where this dish remains very popular, dried oregano and perhaps some fresh tomato chopped in small pieces are also added.

For the basic *bruschetta*: grill the sliced bread, rub it with the clove of garlic and drizzle with olive oil.

Salads

Below are two time-honoured olive dishes eaten in Greece and southern Italy. Olives were part of the daily diet of the peasants, typically eaten with bread. My recipe comes from Sicily, where farm workers used to eat it at the end of a hard day's work, accompanied by fresh durum wheat bread. The preparation is called *olive cunzate* which means 'seasoned olives' in Sicilian dialect. Today *olive cunzate* are normally served as an appetizer, and many cooks can them so they can be eaten during the winter. The olives must be picked green, split and allowed to rest for several months in the brine before they are seasoned.

Green Salad with Olives
Makes 2 cups (500 g)

12 oz. (350 g) cured green olives
½ small red onion, sliced
1 stalk celery with some tender leaves, chopped
1 carrot, thinly sliced
1 garlic clove, minced
2 tbsp (30 g) dried oregano
1 small hot pepper, chopped
2 tbsp (30 ml) wine vinegar
2 tbsp (30 ml) olive oil

Rinse the olives to remove excess salt, and shake them dry. Put the olives in a bowl with the onion, celery, garlic, oregano, and hot pepper. Mix with the vinegar and olive oil. Serve at room temperature. Serves 5

Roasted Black Olives with Orange Zest
Makes 2 cups

12 oz. pound (350 g) oil-cured black olives
pinch of brown sugar
1 teaspoon rosemary needles
grated peel of 1 orange
2 garlic cloves, crushed
1 small chilli pepper, chopped
½ cup olive oil

Strain the olives from the olive oil, add a small dash of olive oil in to the pan. Then heat them in the pan for at least 5 minutes until they get nice and shiny. Transfer the olives to a bowl and stir in the brown sugar, rosemary, orange peel, garlic and pepper. Serve lukewarm.
Serves 4

Caponata (Sicilian aubergine salad)
—from Anna Tasca Lanza, *The Heart of Sicily*

Caponata, often called 'Sicilian caviar', is one of the most celebrated dishes of the island's cuisine. The origins of caponata are unknown, but the preparation belongs to a large family of aubergine dishes such as ratatouille from the South of France or moussaka from Greece. What makes this Sicilian preparation special is the sweet and sour flavouring, which belongs to Sicilian culinary tradition and goes back to ancient Roman tastes, when the seasoning was made of the fish sauce *garum* and honey.

2 lb (1 kg) aubergines (eggplants), peeled and cut into 1-inch cubes
oil for frying
salt
1 large onion, sliced lengthwise
¼ cup (60 ml) olive oil
1 ½ cups (375 ml) tomato sauce, plus more if necessary

1 bunch celery, tough outer ribs discarded, strings removed and
coarsely sliced, then poached
6 oz. (¾ to 1 cup,170 g) green olives, stoned and cut into thirds
4 tbsp (60 g) capers, rinsed and drained
1 tbsp (15 g) sugar, plus more to taste
¼ cup (60 ml) wine vinegar
hard-boiled eggs, peeled and halved, for garnish
chopped parsley for garnish

Heat one inch of oil in a large sauté pan. Fry the aubergine pieces, a batch at a time, until browned. Drain well on paper towels. Season with salt.

Sauté the onion in the olive oil for about 5 minutes, until just golden. Add the celery, olives, capers, tomato sauce, sugar, vinegar and salt to taste. Gently stir in the aubergine, being careful not to break it up. Simmer for 2 to 3 minutes, then transfer to a large bowl or platter and cool.

Pile the caponata in a pyramid and surround it with hard-boiled eggs, sprinkle with chopped parsley, and serve cold or at room temperature. It is even better if made a day before serving. Serves 8 to 10

Sauces and Seasonings Made with Olive Oil

Pesto

Ask a Genoese for a recipe for pesto and you will get . . . not a recipe, but suggestions!

'I'm afraid I just do it all by eye', says my friend Maria Flora, based on the consistency of the bunches of basil, the ones with the small, pointed leaves, from Pra' or the western Ligurian Riviera – they vary depending on the season.

In short, pesto is a question of balance and taste. It's like tomato sauce for southern Italians: everyone has his or her own recipe; there are hundreds of them, and it's all a question of balancing the ingredients to taste.

For 4 people: 4 large bunches of basil

Clean the leaves by hand, rinse and dry them delicately. You can use the blender, the mixer or chop the leaves with a knife; once upon a time pesto was made in the mortar. Before starting to work on the basil, prepare: 4 or 5 spoonfuls of grated parmesan cheese and 1 tbs of aged *pecorino*, grated, 100 gr. Italian pine nuts (don't use imported Chinese pine nuts, they are tasteless), one clove of garlic without the green fillet. Add the basil leaves with a pinch or two of salt to prevent the basil from turning black. The liquid in the basil will be absorbed by the grated cheeses. Taste to adjust the salt; pecorino is very salty. Blend all the ingredients with extra virgin olive oil. Serve *trenette* or *linguine* pasta with the pesto, adding, to the cooking water, one small potato and a small bunch of green beans per person. Bring the water to the boil, toss in the green beans, and when they are cooked, put in the pasta and the potato chopped into cubes.

Now stir some of the water from the boiling pasta into the pesto. Drain the pasta, put it in another bowl, and pour over the pesto sauce. Keep the pesto on top; if the hot pasta sits on the sauce, it can melt the cheese. Add some extra virgin olive oil if needed. Pesto is also delicious on potato *gnocchi* and in minestrone (with simple *taglierini pasta* made of flour, water and salt): when the soup is cooked, add 2 or 3 tbsp of pesto.

Bagna cauda

Bagna cauda is an eighteenth-century recipe from the Piedmont region of northwest Italy. It's a perfect demonstration of the fact that cuisine is often the result of trade and exchange between different cultures. In fact two ingredients of this sauce – the anchovies and the olive oil – are not native to Piedmont. They are Ligurian, although it should be noted that once upon a time olive trees also grew in Piedmont. This dish is the result of trade between Ligurian fishermen and Piedmontese farmers. The fisherman would come up the Piedmontese valleys to exchange salt and salted fish for garlic, butter, cheese and vegetables from Piedmont. *Bagna cauda* was traditionally eaten to celebrate the end of the grape harvest and the new wine. It is first recorded in a recipe book of 1766, *Il cuoco piemontese perfezionato a Parigi* (The Piedmontese Cook with the Paris Touch), where it was called 'the sauce known as the "poor man's"'. The poor Piedmontese peasant's diet usually consisted of what little grew in his garden and what he could swap with others. Once upon a time, the only vegetable he had to dip in the sauce were cardoons (white cardoon from Chieri or around Asti).

¾ of a head of garlic per person
50 g anchovies
750 ml olive oil
butter
salt, cardoons, peppers, Jerusalem artichokes, cabbage,
turnips, beetroot etc.

Break the garlic into cloves, peel and remove any green shoots inside. Place it in a pot, cover with milk and cook until soft (use the point of a knife to test). Discard the milk, place the garlic on a cutting board and chop roughly. Sprinkle with fine salt and continue chopping until finely chopped. Place the garlic in oil. Desalt the anchovies, rinse them in vinegar, dry and chop finely, then add to the oil and garlic. Heat over a low flame, without allowing the oil to come to a boil, stirring continuously, until the mixture is fairly homogeneous. After about 20 minutes, dissolve small pieces of butter in the *bagna cauda*, and when the butter has melted, send the sauce to the table, keeping it warm over a spirit flame without allowing it to come to the boil. Dip the vegetables, finely sliced, into the *bagna cauda*.

Aioli

Aioli is basically a mayonnaise made with garlic. One of the most popular Provençal recipes, it is usually served with poached vegetables.

6 fresh garlic cloves
2 egg yolks at room temperature
pinch of salt
1 cup (225 ml) extra virgin olive oil

Mash the garlic in a mortar to a paste. Add the salt and one egg yolk. Stir slowly but firmly, add the second yolk and stir again evenly. Add the oil drop by drop until the mixture thickens. When the aioli holds the fork upright it is ready. Serves 4 people. Makes 1 cup.

Olive Pastes

Together with *bruschetta*, olive paste is one of the most ancient and popular recipes using olives in the Mediterranean world. It was apparently sold by street vendors in ancient Athens and served as an appetizer (*gustatio*) in Roman banquets. Columella records a recipe for olive paste made out of very ripe black olives cured with salt and seasoned with fenugreek, cumin, fennel seed and Egyptian anise. The name *tapenade*, which is the Provençal version, comes from the word *tapéno*, which in Provençal means capers, one of the main ingredients. Traditionally, *tapenade* is spread on bread or used as a topping for pasta. Although olive paste is known as a Provençal dish, olives are eaten wherever olives grow, and the varieties of olive paste are as widespread as the ingredients which grow around the Mediterranean Sea. Along with *tapenade*, I'd like to suggest an Israeli recipe that probably dates back to Biblical times. What makes this recipe special is the addition of citron, a sacred fruit for the Jews, along with some other spices that give this dish a flavour far more oriental than the French *tapenade*.

Black Olive Paste

450 g pitted black olives
3 tbsp olive oil
1 garlic clove
1 tbsp lemon or citron juice
pinch of cumin, marjoram, parsley and fresh coriander, minced

Grind all the ingredients to a paste in a mortar with pestle, drizzle in the oil and mix until creamy. Refrigerate overnight and serve at room temperature.

Tapenade

½ pound (225 g) green or Kalamata olives
1 ½ tbsp drained capers
2–6 anchovy fillets
2 tbsp olive oil
2 large cloves of garlic, minced or pressed
dash fresh lemon juice
thyme, rosemary and black pepper to taste

Follow instructions for Black Olive Paste above.

Main Dishes and Side Dishes

Olive ascolane

The most typical dish from the Marches region in Italy, a region with extensive olive groves. The recipe, named after the capital of the region, Ascoli, is an old one that dates back to the end of the nineteenth century. Tender olives preserved in brine with wild fennel seeds and various aromatic local herbs, are stuffed with veal, pork and *prosciutto crudo*, along with parmesan cheese and various spices.

1 kg green olives from Ascoli
150 g minced veal meat
150 g minced pork meat
100 g *prosciutto crudo*
50 g grated pecorino
50 g grated parmesan
4 eggs
tomato paste
breadcrumbs
flour
nutmeg
½ glass white wine
olive oil, salt and pepper to taste

Brown the veal and pork in oil in a pan, add salt and pepper and sprinkle with the white wine. When the wine has evaporated, cover the pan and allow the meat to cook through. Place the pork and veal in a bowl and add the finely chopped *prosciutto*, the grated cheeses, some breadcrumbs, a pinch of nutmeg, the tomato paste and two eggs. Mix well to form a smooth, thick paste. Pit the olives and stuff them with the mixture, then roll them in flour, pass them in the remaining two eggs, beaten, and roll in breadcrumbs. Cook them in very hot oil to cover and serve hot.

Artichoke Hearts and Broad Beans in Oil
—from Claudia Roden, *A New Book of Middle Eastern Food*

This is a Copt recipe eaten during Lent, when these Christians abstain from any kind of animal food.

6 artichokes
juice of 1 lemon
2–3 tbsp olive oil
1 clove garlic
1 tsp sugar
1 lb (500 g) fresh shelled or frozen broad beans

salt and black pepper
1 tbsp flour or cornflour

Buy young artichokes, and remove the leaves, stems and chokes. Use only the hearts. Rub with lemon juice and drop in 150 ml (¼ pint) water acidulated with lemon to prevent discoloration.

Put the olive oil, garlic, sugar and lemon water in a large pan with the artichoke hearts. Add the broad beans, and season to taste with salt and pepper. Add more water to cover if necessary. Simmer gently over low heat for about 45 minutes, until the artichoke hearts and beans are very tender and the liquid is considerably reduced.

Mix the flour or cornflour to a smooth paste with a little cold water. Add a little of the hot liquid and stir well. Then add this to the pan gradually stirring constantly. Simmer gently, stirring occasionally until the sauce thickens and has lost the taste of flour (about 15 minutes). Pour into a serving dish.

Serve hot as a side dish.

Moroccan Chicken with Cracked Green Olives
—from Maggie Blyth Klein, *The Feast of Olives*

2 cups (500 g) cracked green olives
4 tbsp (60 ml) olive oil
1 chicken (4 lb or 1.8 kg)
salt and pepper to taste
1 tsp fresh ginger, minced
3 cloves garlic, minced
1 tbsp cumin seeds, finely ground in a mortar
large pinch of saffron threads, crushed
2 ½ cups (560 ml) chicken stock, preferably homemade
red-leaf lettuce leaves or curly endive
¼ cup (60 ml) fresh lemon juice
grated zest of one lemon

Stone the olives, then place in a sauce pan with water to cover. Bring to a boil and boil for 15 minutes. Drain and repeat with fresh water, then drain again (this boiling process makes the olives less bitter, but dulls their bright green colour). Set aside.

In a large heavy casserole over medium-high heat, warm 2 tbsp of the olive oil. Add the whole chicken and brown well on all sides, about 15 minutes. Remove from the pan and sprinkle with salt and pepper. Set aside.

Drain off the fat from the pan. Warm the remaining 2 tbsp oil in the same pan over medium heat. Add the ginger, garlic, cumin and saffron and sauté for 1 minute. Then add the chicken stock and stir well.

Return the chicken to the pot, cover and cook for 12 minutes on one side. Turn the chicken over, re-cover, and cook for 12 minutes on the other side. The chicken should be just done; test by piercing with a knife tip. If it is not ready, cook for a few more minutes, and test again.

Arrange a bed of lettuce on a serving platter. Remove the chicken from the liquid and place it on the lettuce. Add the lemon juice to the liquid in the pot and reduce over high heat until the sauce is slightly thickened. Add the olives and heat just long enough to warm them through. Using a slotted spoon, distribute the olives over the chicken.

Pour the sauce into a bowl and serve alongside the chicken. Garnish the chicken with the lemon zest.
Serves 4

Spaghetti aglio, olio e peperoncino

'Spaghetti aglio, olio e peperoncino', spaghetti with oil, garlic and chilli, is universally Italian. It is by far the most popular dish of pasta in southern Italian families. This is a last-minute dish you can whip up on your return from a weekend out of town, when the refrigerator is empty. No Italian home is ever without the ingredients.

There are two schools of thought about the garlic: those who fry it in the oil and those who like to add it raw. My only rule is to be sure all the ingredients are fresh. You cannot make this pasta with stale garlic and the olive oil must have a pungent taste; in fact, new olive oil is perfect. Rather than dictate fixed amounts of ingredients, let me just give you the overall picture. I would chop a couple of cloves of garlic and 1 small chilli pepper together and let them simmer in a cup of olive oil for at least an hour. Then, after the pasta has been cooked and drained, I would pour it into a bowl with the seasoned oil, and stir. Eventually I might add a tablespoon of grated pecorino. That's it!

Broccoli with Black Olives
—from Anna Tasca Lanza, *The Heart of Sicily*

around 2 lb (1 kg) broccoli
1 small onion, minced
½ cup (125 ml) olive oil
½ cup (75 g) cured black olives, stoned and sliced
salt
black pepper
½ cup (50 g) grated pecorino or parmesan
½ lb (250 g) mozzarella, shredded (optional)

Cut the broccoli into 5-cm (2-inch) florets and boil in well-salted water until *al dente*, about 5 minutes, then drain. Meanwhile, sauté the onion in half the olive oil until slightly golden, 2 to 3 minutes. Remove the pan from the heat and add the olives. Set the mixture aside.

Preheat the oven to 190°C/375°F. Oil an 8 x 12 inch baking dish with about 1 tbsp of the olive oil.

Spread out the broccoli in the dish and mix in the onion and olive mixture. Add the remaining olive oil, if desired. Add salt and pepper, remembering that the olives and the cheese you will be adding may be salty. Toss the broccoli with about half of the pecorino and top with mozzarella, if desired. Sprinkle the remaining pecorino on top. Bake for about 20 to 30 minutes, until the top is nice and golden. Serve warm or at room temperature.
Serves 4 to 6 as a side dish

Olive Focaccia

For the dough:
3 ½ cups (500 g) semolina flour
1 ½ tbsp (12 g) fresh yeast
1 cup (190 ml) water
½ cup (125 ml) olive oil
½ cup (125 ml) white wine
½ tbsp salt
For the topping:
¾ cup (100 g) black olives, stoned
2 sprigs rosemary
drizzle olive oil
pinch of sea salt

Make a well in the flour, add the yeast, and start adding water (about 70 ml) to dissolve the yeast, mixing with your hands. Mix in the olive oil until incorporated, then mix in the wine until incorporated, and add more water. Add the salt and add more water if necessary. Knead the dough for about 8 minutes (it will be quite sticky), then transfer to a large oiled bowl and let rise, covered with a towel, in a warm place for about 30 minutes.

Preheat oven to 200°C.

Place the dough in a large round springform pans and let rise for another 10 minutes. Pat dough with your fingertips to make dimples in the dough. Place pitted olives on dough, sprinkle with rosemary and sea salt, and drizzle with olive oil. Bake for about 40 minutes, until golden.

Moroccan Lamb Tagine with Prunes and Olives
—from Maggie Blyth Klein, *The Feast of Olives*

This is a typical Moroccan tagine with its sweet and sour flavour that emerges from the contrast between the prunes and the bitterness of green olives. You serve it over bulgur wheat or couscous.

3 tbsp olive oil
3 lb (2.7 kg) lamb shoulder, trimmed of fat and
cut into bite-size pieces
1 tsp salt
pinch of saffron threads, crushed
good pinch of cayenne pepper
1 heaped tsp finely chopped fresh ginger
½ teaspoon ground cinnamon
1 yellow onion, half minced and half thinly sliced
2 cloves of garlic peeled and chopped
¾ cup large brine-cured black olives, Moroccan or Amfissa for
preference
½ pound (225 g) prunes, pitted and plumped in warm water
1 tbsp sesame seeds, lightly toasted
1 ½ tsp honey
1 bunch fresh coriander, chopped
2 tbsp unsalted butter
2 tart apples, peeled, cored and sliced

Warm the olive oil in a heavy casserole over medium-high heat,.
Add the lamb and sauté, using tongs to turn the pieces so that they
brown on all surfaces. Add the salt, saffron, cayenne, ginger, cinnamon, minced onion, garlic and water to cover. Stir well, bring
to a simmer and cover and cook over medium-low heat until tender,
about 1 hour.

Add the olives, prunes, sesame seeds, honey, coriander leaves,
and sliced onion and stir well. Re-cover and continue to simmer
for 5 minutes to blend the flavours. Meanwhile, in a a skillet over
medium heat, melt the butter. Add the apple slices and sauté, turning once, until soft, about 10 minutes total cooking time. Transfer
to a serving dish and decorate with the sliced apples.

Serves 8

Melomakarona (or Phoenika)
—from Lynn Alley, *Lost Arts*

These are traditional Greek Christmas cookies. They are some-times called *phoenika* after the Phoenicians, who arrived in Greece and Sicily around the eighth century BCE. Today, some cooks prefer to substitute butter for olive oil. But once upon a time, the fat used was always olive oil. This recipe makes approximately two dozen cookies.

Cookies
3 ¼ cup (450 g) plain (all purpose) flour
1 ½ cup (210 g) semolina flour
⅓ cup (70 g) sugar
2 tsp baking powder
zest from 1 orange, zest from 1 lemon
1 tsp ground cloves
1 tsp ground cinnamon
1 cup olive oil
1 cup fresh orange juice
½ cup (110 ml) brandy

Sugar syrup
1 cup (200 g) sugar
1 cup (350 g) honey
2 cups (450 ml) water
1 stick cinnamon
6 whole cloves
1 whole nutmeg, crushed
1 strip orange peel
1 strip lemon peel

Topping
1 cup (115 g) chopped walnuts
2 tsp finely ground cloves

Mix the dough by combining the flour with the semolina, sugar, baking powder, grated citrus rinds and spices with olive oil, orange juice and brandy. Shape the dough into a ball, cover it and let it sit for half an hour. Preheat the oven to 190°C/350°F. Take a table-spoonful of dough and shape it into a an oval cookie, place it on a cookie sheet and lightly press with a fork. Bake for 25 minutes or until lightly browned.

While the cookies are baking combine the sugar, honey, water, spices and citrus peel in a sauce pan and bring to a boil. Simmer for about 10 minutes, until the mixture is somewhat thick. Strain the sugar syrup and place in a bowl. Remove the cookies from the oven and allow them to cool completely. Dip each cookie quickly in the sugar syrup and place on the cookie sheet. Quickly sprinkle with chopped walnuts and ground cloves.

Cassatelle

This is one of the most popular cookies from the eastern part of Sicily. It was a sweet for hard times, when ordinary people didn't have much to eat and had to make do with the few ingredients to hand. Ricotta was always considered the cheese of the poor because it was obtained from the whey left over from cow's or ewe's milk after the curd had been extracted to make the primary cheese. The whey was ri-cotta, or 're-cooked', and thus yielded the familiar creamy cheese. The pastry, too, is made of surprisingly simple ingredients, but it is also delicious! It is important to use plentiful oil in the frying.

1 ½ cups (375 ml) white wine
½ cup (125 ml) olive oil
1 lb (500 g) semolina flour
pinch of salt
½ pound (250 g) ricotta
6 tbsp (90 g) sugar
1 tbsp (15 g) cinnamon, plus more for garnish
icing (confectioner's) sugar, for garnish

Heat the wine and oil together until warm (not hot). Pile up the flour and make a well in the centre. Add the wine-oil mixture and salt, then carefully work it in and knead together.

Stir together the ricotta, sugar and cinnamon, and set aside.

Take a piece of the dough and put it through a pasta machine on the widest setting. Roll the dough through the machine about 5 times at this setting, folding the dough in half before rolling it. When it is very smooth, move the dial to the next narrower setting and roll it through 2 to 3 times more, folding it before rolling it. Move the dial to the third setting and roll it through 2 or 3 more times.

On a floured work surface, lay out the sheet of dough and cut out circles with a 10-cm (3 ¾-inch) cookie cutter. Place a spoonful of ricotta filling just off-centre, then moisten edges of dough and fold over. Pinch to seal. Repeat with remaining dough and filling.

Heat 4 cm (1 ½ inches) of olive oil and deep-fry the cookies, flipping occasionally, until deep golden, about 3 minutes. Drain on paper towels, then sprinkle with the icing sugar and cinnamon. Serve warm.

Appendix: Olive Varieties

There are hundreds of different varieties of olive trees. Some cultivars are very closely related, almost identical, distinguished only by their slightly different names; some vary one from another much more widely. At times a single variety may be known by different names in different places, even within one country. Olives vary according to their appearance, growing characteristics, size, oil content, taste, chemical qualities, ripening time and many other factors. I have listed only a few varieties per country.

Spain

Arbequina, a small, golden-brown olive from Catalogna, is used as a table olive and for olive oil, which has a buttery and peppery aroma.

Cornicabra, from Castille and Mancha, produces a strong, aromatic oil with a distinct bitterness and a suggestion of pepper in its bite.

Empeltre is a medium-sized black olive from Aragon, used both as a table olive and to produce a high-quality olive oil. It has a ripe, red apple and fresh fruit aroma.

Empeltre (ii), mostly grown in Catalonia, is used for olive oil as well as black table olives. It has a sweet taste with aromas of fresh fruit and almonds.

Hojiblanca, or 'white leaf' in Spanish, is a green to purple medium-sized olive with firm pulp from Andalusia. Rich in vegetable flavour, it is used to make olive oil despite its low oil content.

Morisca, from Estremadura, is a highly productive variety, with big pulpy fruit and a high oil content. It is also used as a green table olive.

Picual, the most important Spanish cultivar, is a medium-sized black olive used to produce olive oil. It has a spicy, fruity and slightly bitter flavour, an aroma of fresh herbs and flowers and a high oil content.

Picudo, a small purple olive, is highly productive and makes excellent olive oil (the one from Baena is considered the best). It is also cured as a table olive.

Italy

Bianca, **Bosana** and **Tonda** olive cultivars from Sardinia produce a green olive oil with a hint of bitterness and aromas of artichoke and dandelion.

Carolea, **Coratina** and **Ogliarota** from Campania produce a dense, fruity and golden olive oil.

Dolce Agogia, from Umbria, is a medium-sized green to purple olive with medium oil content; it is used also to make sun-dried black olives.

Frantoio, a cultivar grown in central Italy, is highly productive and makes a very fruity olive oil.

Leccino, grown in Umbria and Tuscany, produces a small black table olive with low oil content.

Moraiolo and **Raggiola**, from Umbria, produce an olive oil with a slightly fruity flavour and a peppery kick; its aroma is reminiscent of artichokes and it has a very smooth, fluid texture.

Nocellara del Belice is a Sicilian variety that is pulpy, green and medium sized. It is excellent for the table and makes good oil.

Taggiasca, a green medium-sized olive from Liguria, produces olive oil with a sweet flavour and delicate texture.

Greece

Kalamata, a large, black olive with a smooth, meaty taste, is used as a table olive.

Portugal

Galega produces olive oil that has a very low natural acidity, delicate texture and flavour reminiscent of fresh fruit and herbs, with aromas ranging from almonds and sugar to spices.

France

Aglandau from Aix-en-Provence produces olive oil with a slight bitterness and an aroma of almonds and hazelnuts.

Cailletier from the Massif de l'Esterel and Nice produces a very refined, light, yellow olive oil with a delicate and slightly sweet flavour and a bouquet reminiscent of almonds, acacia and hawthorn.

Rougette from Ardeche produces a very distinctive olive oil with a woodland aroma and slightly herbal flavour with a suggestion of fruits.

Picholine and **Sabina** from Corsica produce a green olive oil with an herbal bouquet slightly suggestive of green vegetables and a peppery, fiery bite.

Croatia

Oblica is a pulpy, green medium-sized olive; it produces an excellent olive oil with a refined texture, and table olives both black and green.

Tunisia

Chemlali de Sfax, Chetoui, Gerboui, Meski, Oueslati: these varieties produce an olive oil that is greenish in colour with a wonderful aroma and a flavour reminiscent of fresh fruit with a tinge of bitterness.

Turkey

Izmir Sofralik is a bright, pulpy, medium-sized green olive and makes a good table olive. This is an old cultivar grown in the region of Smyrna.

Memecik, a medium-sized olive grown, is used as a table olive and for olive oil. It has a high oil content and is very fruity.

Israel and Palestine

Nabali from Galilee and Israel is one of the oldest olive cultivars in the Middle East, sometimes called the 'Roman' olive. It is used both as a table olive and for oil. The olives, which have a high oil content, are plump and soft.

United States

Mission olives, from California and Texas, are oval and medium in size. The skin of the Mission olive turns deep purple but changes to jet-black when ripe. It is used both for pressing of oil and as a table olive.

Chile

Azapena or **Sevillana de Azapa** can range in size from medium to large and may be picked as a green olive but is most often violet black when harvested for the table. The fruit has an elongated shape and a thin outer skin covering a very fleshy inner meat. It is grown as a table olive to be served as a complement to food.

References

1 The Ancient Roots of the Olive

1 Sandro Vannucci, 'Storia dell'olio', in *L'ulivo e l'olio* (Milano, 2009), pp. 26–71.
2 Maggie Blyth Klein, *The Feast of the Olives: Cooking with Olives and Olive Oil* (San Francisco, CA, 1994), p. 3.
3 Vannucci, 'Storia dell'olio', p. 32.
4 Pliny the Elder, *The Natural History*, ed. John Bostock and H. T. Riley (London, 1855), Book XV, chap. 3.
5 Vannucci, 'Storia dell'olio', p. 44.
6 Massimo Montanari, 'Il sacro e il quotidiano. La cultura dell'olio nel Medioevo europeo', in *Il dono e la quiete il mare verde dell'olio*, ed. Paolo Anelli (Perugia, 1999), pp. 71–4 and Massimo Montanari, 'Olio e vino, due indicatori culturali', in *Olio e vino nell'alto Medioevo* (Spoleto, 2007), pp. 1460.
7 Massimo Mazzotti, 'Enlightened Mills: Mechanizing Olive Oil Production in Mediterranean Europe', *Society for the History of Technology*, 45 (2004), pp. 277–304.

2 Ointment, Anointments and Holy Oil: The Olive in Ritual

1 Fernand Braudel, *The Mediterranean and the Mediterranean World in the Age of Philip II* (London, 1972), p. 24.

2 Giancarlo Baronti, *L'olio e l'olivo nelle tradizioni popolari*,
   Museo dell'Olio e dell'Olivo (Perugia, 2001), p. 124.
3 John Boardman, 'The Olive in the Mediterranean: Its
   Culture and Use', *Philosophical Transactions of the Royal Society*,
   London, 275 (1976), p. 192.
4 Columella, *On Agriculture*, 3 vols, trans. Harrison Boyd Ash,
   E. S. Forster and Edward H. Heffner (Boston, 1941–55).
5 Paolo Branca, '"E fa crescer per voi… l'olivo… e le viti e
   ogni specie di frutti": Vino e olio nella civiltà Arabo-
   Mussulmana' in *Olio e vino nell'alto Medioevo* (Spoleto, 2007),
   pp. 671–706.
6 Cristina Acidini Luchinat, 'Olivo e olive. Immagini
   dall'Antichità al Rinascimento', in *Olivo, tesoro del mediterraneo*
   (Florence, 2004), p. 139.
7 Maguelonne Toussaint-Samat, *History of Food*, trans. Anthea
   Bell (Oxford, 1997), p. 215.
8 Claudia Roden, *A New Book of Middle Eastern Food*
   (London, 1986), p. 352.

3 Harvesting, Pressing and Curing

1 Andrew Dalby, *Cato: On Farming* (Totnes, Devon, 1998),
   chap. 80.
2 Don and Patricia Brothwell, *Food in Antiquity: A Survey of the
   Diet of Early Peoples* (London, 1969), p.
3 Antonio Carpuso and Sara De Fano, *L'olio di oliva dal mito
   alla scienza* (Roma, 1998), p.
4 Maguelonne Toussaint-Samat, *A History of Food,* trans.
   Anthea Bell (Oxford, 1994), p. 216.
5 Dalby, *Cato: On Farming*, ch. 64.
6 Pliny the Elder, *The Natural History*, ed. John Bostock and
   H. T. Riley (London, 1855), book xv.
7 Cato and Varro, *On Agriculture*, trans. W. D. Hooper and
   Harrison Boyd Ash (Boston, 1934).
8 Archestrato di Gela, *I piaceri della mensa (frammenti 330 a.C.)*
   (Palermo, 1987), p. 43.

9 Dalby, *Cato: On Farming*, chap. 119.
10 Brothwell and Brothwell, *Food in Antiquity*, p. 46.
11 Maggie Blyth Klein, *The Feast of the Olives: Cooking with Olives and Olive Oil* (San Francisco, CA, 1994), p. 13.
12 Giovanni Enrico Agosteo, 'La manifattura dell'olio d'oliva in Sicilia: dalla raccolta delle olive all'estrazione dell'olio', in *La Sicilia dell'olio* (Catania, 2008), pp. 143–6.
13 Jean-Louis Flandrin, 'Le gout et la nécessité: sur l'usage des graisses dans les cuisine d'Europe occidentale (XIV–XVIII)', in *Annales Économies, Sociétés, Civilisations*, 38 (1983), pp. 369–401.

4 The Olive Meets the New World

1 Judith M. Taylor MD, *The Olive in California: History of an Immigrant Tree* (Berkeley, CA, 2000), p. 25.
2 Simone Cinotto, *Una famiglia che mangia insieme, cibo ed eticità nella comunità italoamericana di New York, 1920–1940* (Turin, 2001), p. 327.
3 Mario Puzo, quoted ibid., p. 2.
4 Ibid., p. 332.
5 Sandro Vannucci, 'Storia dell'olio', in *L'ulivo e l'olio* (Milano, 2009), p. 66.
6 Maggie Blyth Klein, *The Feast of the Olives, Cooking with Olives and Olive Oil* (San Francisco, CA, 1994), pp. 18–19.
7 Mort Rosenblum, *Olives: The Life and Lore of a Noble Fruit* (New York, 1997), p. 290.
8 Taylor, *The Olive in California*, pp. 50–51.
9 Ibid., p.55.

5 Good Fat and Bad Fat: The Mediterranean Diet

1 Simone Cinotto, *Una famiglia che mangia insieme, cibo ed eticità nella comunità italoamericana di New York, 1920–1940* (Turin,

2001), p. 157.

2 Anne Meneley, 'Like an Extra Virgin', *American Anthropologist*, CIX/4 (2007), p. 679.

3 Piero Camporesi, *Le vie del latte* (Milan, 1993), pp. 107–8.

4 Meneley, 'Like an Extra Virgin', p. 679. Certainly, as Dr Daphne Miller writes, the high polyphenol content of olive oil can partially explain why it is so heart healthy. But Lluís Serra-Majem PhD, a researcher at the University of Barcelona in Spain, offers some additional reasons why olive oil is so terrific for your health. After administering diet questionnaires to 1,600 adults in Spain, he discovered that people who ate a lot of olive oil were more likely to eat green vegetables, whole grains and fish while people who steered away from olive oil were more likely to eat sweets, processed cereals, refined breads and foods high in refined vegetable oils and animal fats. What did this mean? Did olive oil just happen to be an innocent bystander in the success of the Cretan diet? Perhaps it was just a food that was preferred by people who happened to make other healthy food choices. See more in Miller, *The Jungle Effect* (New York, 2008), p. 119.

5 David Kamp, *The United States of Arugula* (New York, 2006), p. 217.

6 Meneley, 'Like an Extra Virgin', p. 679.

7 'Olive Oil Sales Boom in UK Shops', *BBC News*, 13 January 2006.

8 The discussion is now shifting on to how fat is made: if cold pressed, organically grown, first press, with no contaminants, or, in the case of animal fat, what they are fed with. See Miller, *The Jungle Effect*.

Select Bibliography

Alley, Lynn, *Lost Arts* (Berkeley, CA, 1995)

Angelici, Renzo, ed., *L'ulivo e l'olio* (Milan, 2009)

Archestrato di Gela, *I piaceri della mensa (frammenti 330 a.C)* (Palermo, 1987)

Boardman, John, 'The Olive in the Mediterranean: Its Culture and Use', *Philosophical Transactions of the Royal Society, London, B*, CCLXXV/187–96 (1976)

Branca, Paolo, '"E fa crescere per voi…l'olivo… e le viti e ogni specie di frutti". Vino e olio nella civiltà arabo-mussulmana', in *Olio e vino nell'alto Medioevo* (Spoleto, 2007)

Braudel, Fernand, *The Mediterranean and the Mediterranean World in the Age of Philip II* (London, 1972)

Brothwell, Don and Patricia, *Food in Antiquity: A Survey of the Diet of Early Peoples* (London, 1969)

Cato and Varro, *On Agriculture*, trans. W. D. Hooper and Harrison Boyd Ash (Boston, MA, 1934)

Carpuso, Antonio and Sara De Fano, *Olive Oil: From Myth to Science* (Rome, 1998)

Caruso, Tiziano, and Gaetano Magnano di San Lio, *La Sicilia dell'olio* (Catania, 2008)

Cinotto, Simone, *Una famiglia che mangia insieme cibo ed etnicità nella comunità italoamericana di New York, 1920–1040* (Turin, 2001)

Ciuffoletti, Zefiro, ed., *Olivo, tesoro del mediterraneo* (Florence, 2004)

Columella, *On Agriculture*, trans Harrison Boyd Ash, E. S. Forster and Edward H. Heffner, 3 vols (Boston, MA, 1941–55)

Dalby, Andrew, *Cato: On Farming* (Totnes, Devon 1998)

Flandrin, Jean-Louis, 'Le gout et la nécessité: sur l'usage des graisses dans les cuisine d'Europe occidentale (XIV–XVIII)', in *Annales Économies, Sociétés, Civilisations*, 38 (1983)

Glazer, Phyllis, *Gusti, alimenti e riti della tavola nell'Antico e nel Nuovo Testamento* (Casale M., 1995)

Klein, Maggie Blyth, *The Feast of the Olive* (San Francisco, CA, 1994)

Knickerbocker, Peggy, *Olive Oil from Tree to Table* (San Francisco, CA, 1997)

Marchetti Lungarotti, Maria Grazia, ed., *Museo dell'olivo e dell'olio* (Torgiano, 2001)

Mazzotti, Massimo, 'Enlightened Mills: Mechanizing Olive Oil Production in Mediterranean Europe', *Society for the History of Technology*, 45 (2004)

Miller, Daphne, *The Jungle Effect* (New York, 2008)

Montanari, Massimo, 'Olio e vino, due indicatori culturali', in *Olio e vino nell'alto Medioevo* (Spoleto, 2007)

Pliny the Elder, *The Natural History*, ed. and trans. John Bostock and H. T. Riley (London, 1855)

Rosenblum, Mort, *Olives: The Life and Lore of a Noble Fruit* (New York, 1996)

Tasca Lanza, Anna, *The Heart of Sicily* (New York, 1993)

Toussaint-Samat, Maguelonne, *History of Food,* trans. Anthea Bell (Oxford, 1997)

Websites and Associations

The Olive Blog
A blog about olives and olive oil
www.theoliveblog.com

The International Olive Council
www.internationaloliveoil.org

The Olive Oil Source
Different varieties of olives
www.oliveoilsource.com/page/olive-varietals

Olive oil cultivars around the world
www.frantoio-bo.it/cultivar.aspx

The Australin Olive Oil Association
www.australianextravirgin.com.au

The Hunter Olive Association, New South Wales
www.hunterolives.asn.au

Associazione Italiana dell'Industria Olearia
www.federalimentare.it/docassitol.html

Indian Olive Association
www.indolive.org

California Olive Assocation
Information about chemicals in olives
http://oehha.ca.gov/Prop65/pdf/BMcFarland%20CA%20Oliv
e%20comment.pdf

Napa Valley Olive Growers
http://napavalleyolivegrowers.com

Acknowledgements

I would like to thank Frederika Randall for her valuable guidance, her suggestions, patient support and meticulous editing; Arlyn Balke, who was at the origin of this passionate olive adventure; Francesca d'Andrea, Mary Taylor Simeti and Kate Wislow for their observations and patience in reading the manuscript; Daphne Miller, Lauren Bennet, Fabio Parasecoli, Giuseppe Barbera and Paolo Inglese for being there when I needed them; Maria Flora Giubilei for her delightful pesto recipe; Guy Ambrosino for his beautiful photos; Domenico Musci for his research on *bagna cauda*; Lynn Alley, Claudia Roden and Maggie Blyth Klein for letting me use some of their recipes; and my father for his unyielding pride in me!

Photo Acknowledgements

The author and the publishers wish to express their thanks to the below sources of illustrative material and/or permission to reproduce it.

Guy Ambrosino: pp. 10, 13, 16, 31, 45, 55, 58, 59, 61, 81, 84; Giuseppe Barbera: p. 24; Bardo Museum, Tunis, Tunisia: p. 79; Bigstock: p. 78 (Anna Smirnova); © Trustees of the British Museum, London: pp. 20, 53; Reproduced from the collection of the Butte County Historical Society, Oroville, California: p. 73; Reproduced from the photograph collection of the California History Section of the California Sate Library, Sacramento, California: p. 72; Indianapolis Museum of Arts, Indianapolis: p. 75; Istockphoto; p. 6 (Juanmonio); Reproduced from the collections of The Library of Congress Prints and Photographs Division, Washington DC: pp. 49, 52, 67; The Metropolitan Museum of Art, New York: p. 85; Museo dell'olivo e dell'Olio, Torgiano, Italy: pp. 9, 14, 33, 36, 38, 39, 43; Museo dell' Opera Metropolitana, Siena, Italy: p. 34; The National Gallery, London: p. 63; Ariane Sallier de la Tour: p. 30; Victoria and Albert Museum, London: p. 83; Yale Center for British Art, New Haven, Connecticut: p. 26.

Index

italic numbers refer to illustrations; **bold** to recipes